MERRITT PROFESSIONAL PUBLISHING

THE QUICK STUDY

THE MARKET CONDUCT HANDBOOK FOR AGENTS

How to Sell Insurance Ethically and Comply with the Law

THIS HANDBOOK BELONGS TO:

NAME

ADDRESS

EDITION

1

MERRITT PROFESSIONAL PUBLISHING

Merritt Professional Publishing publishes many insurance and safety educational materials. For more information call TOLL-FREE: 800-638-7597.

Written By

Cynthia Davidson, CIC

Editors

Tracy Lovik, J.D.
Donald Schlossman
Richard Morin, CIC

Production

Simone Hirzel

Merritt Professional Publishing
1661 Ninth Street/P.O. Box 955
Santa Monica, California 90406

ISBN 1-56343-123-

B-7465(210)97 1 2M

ACKNOWLEDGMENTS

This project would not have been possible without the assistance and cooperation of the state regulators and insurance industry representatives who agreed to speak openly with us and share their expertise on the topic of market conduct.

Special thanks are in order for:

Al Dawson, Managing Counsel, American Council of Life Insurance

Kay Doughty, Doughty Market Conduct & Regulatory Consulting, Arlington, Texas

John Mancini, Market Affairs Manager, National Association of Insurance Commissioners

Gene Reed, Delaware Insurance Department

Warren Spruill, Virginia Insurance Department

Martin Wilson, Troutman Sanders Law Firm, Atlanta, Georgia

The Merritt Editors who contributed to this book include Tracy Lovik, Don Schlossman and Ericka Weeks. Thanks also to Simone Hirzel, Ginger McKelvey, and Cesar Flores.

CONTENTS

CHAPTER 3
THE AGENT'S RESPONSIBILITIES TO THE INSURANCE COMPANY

CHAPTER 4
THE INSURER'S RESPONSIBILITIES TO POLICYHOLDERS

INTRODUCTION

The New Focus on Market Conduct

Among the insurance industry's most prominent challenges are allegations of wrongful conduct by agents and companies selling insurance, accompanied by million dollar settlements, negative publicity, plummeting consumer confidence in the industry, and a new regulatory focus on "market conduct".

In 1994 Metropolitan Life paid out almost $100 million in restitutions and fines to settle accusations of deceptive sales practices by agents. In 1995 New York Life settled a class action suit for an estimated $65 million, based on charges of misleading policy illustrations. In early 1996, New York regulators fined John Hancock Mutual Life Insurance Company $1 million for alleged churning of policies and use of misleading advertising. (The violations took place between 1983 and 1994.) A multi-state task force of more than two dozen state regulators was formed in 1995 solely to investigate sales practices and allegations of churning at the Prudential. The result: the largest fine ever against a U.S. insurance company — $35 million.

These insurers are hardly alone; the list of companies facing market misconduct charges continues to grow. Headlines accuse agents and companies alike of:

- ✔ Deceptive sales practices
- ✔ Misleading policy illustrations
- ✔ Churning
- ✔ Twisting
- ✔ Vanishing premiums that do not vanish
- ✔ Misrepresentation of policy characteristics
- ✔ Unnecessary replacement
- ✔ Unfair discrimination
- ✔ Predatory pricing
- ✔ Unfair underwriting practices
- ✔ Redlining, and
- ✔ Other instances of consumer abuse

Hearings on deceptive sales tactics in the insurance industry have been held by the House Subcommittee on Commerce, Consumer Protection, and Competitiveness. There is concern that the national attention being paid to market conduct may rekindle efforts to replace state oversight of the insurance industry with federal oversight. One insurance association warned that a lack of industry response could invite "Congressional intervention if high profile market conduct problems continue unabated."

The lawsuits and public relations fallout have damaged the whole industry. Despite studies showing that consumers give their own agents high ratings, the industry as a whole is suffering a credibility crisis. According to research by the American Council of Life Insurance (ACLI), in 1994 only 24% of Americans agreed that life insurance companies had high ethical standards (down from 50% in 1968); and only 18% felt life insurers were "honest in dealing with their customers" (as opposed to 37% as recently as 1986).

Industry experts predict that market conduct will take on even greater significance in the coming years, especially with regard to policy illustrations and full disclosure at the time the policy is sold.

It remains to be seen how creatively the industry will respond to this new focus on market conduct, but already the more proactive companies are beefing up their compliance departments, conducting internal market conduct exams, randomly surveying customers, and taking such issues as their advertising materials much more seriously. A representative from MetLife (whose market conduct practices were among the first to be scrutinized) says "nothing comes out of the marketing department anymore without a code stamp indicating approval by the legal department."

In the March 1996 edition of *Best's Review, Life/Health*, editor Ellen Friedman-Kelly writes, "Someone can always find a way around the regulations. The challenge for company leadership is integrating market conduct into the corporate value system and making it a driving force of the corporate culture.... It takes courage to look beyond compliance and deal with an intangible like market conduct as a corporate value."

Who is Responsible?

Who is responsible for deceptive sales practices? Are abusive practices the work of a few scattered agents or is there evidence of systematic wrongdoing (and systemic flaws) at insurance company home offices? Insurers have historically allowed their insurance agents great flexibility in sales practices; however, recent class action lawsuits suggest that sustained abuses by numerous agents over a long period of time may indicate that home offices tolerate and perhaps even encourage improper sales activities.

Some contend it is the company's lower level sales managers, whose pay is based on the sales production of the agents they supervise, that encourage deceptive sales practices. Sales materials and techniques developed in the field may not be authorized and may in fact be in violation of company policy — and state law.

In the fallout after one market conduct investigation, agents claimed that company managers had destroyed the marketing and sales documents that were the subject of a regulatory probe, and had purged office computers of software that violated state and federal regulations. Agents who were dismissed for using deceptive sales practices protested that the sales pitches they used were taught to them by company managers.

State regulators have concluded that the use of misleading advertising and sales materials demonstrates an inadequate control by the company over the content, form, and method of distribution of its advertisements. Many home offices have now prohibited the use of any sales and marketing materials unless they have first received approval from the home office. Insurers have flooded their sales offices with memos on acceptable sales practices, revised compliance and training programs, and increased field auditing.

Compliance Redefined

One thing is clear: regardless of where the fault directly lies, responsibility for compliance is being redefined from the field to the home office. The standards by which individuals and companies are being held accountable have changed. Increasingly, insurance companies are being held responsible for the actions of their agents, to the tune of millions of dollars in fines. And agents are being held responsible for their conduct in the field through license revocations and in some cases, criminal prosecution.

The executive summary of the multi-state Prudential examination lays the blame for breaches of compliance squarely on company management. "Prudential is responsible for the behavior of its agents and managers and, therefore, where misrepresentations have resulted in harm to its customers, the company should provide appropriate compensation commensurate with the nature and amount of the harm and misrepresentation."

Where Agents Fit In

The tangle of state regulations, accepted industry practice, and home office guidelines can be bewildering for agents. What was last year's top sales approach may now be grounds for termination of agent appointment. One state's unfair trade practice may be considered healthy competition somewhere else.

This book is intended to serve as a guide to market conduct issues for insurance agents, so that they understand their legal, professional, and ethical obligations to both policyholders and to the insurance company(ies) they represent. It is also intended to inform agents of the types of support they may expect from insurers, and help them provide the best possible service to the insurance-buying public. Whether you are a new agent or a seasoned professional, you are your own best defense against these entanglements.

As an added benefit, agents may be able to use this text to help satisfy state continuing education requirements for agent license renewal. To do so, the agent must complete and pass a written examination based on the text materials and score 70% or better. In most cases, the exam must be taken in a proctored, closed-book setting.

Note: Despite our best efforts, it is possible that charts summarizing specific regulations in all states may omit details or state exceptions. To be sure about a particular provision, please refer to the state insurance code or contact the state insurance department directly.

CHAPTER 1

UNDERSTANDING MARKET CONDUCT

Market conduct, simply defined, is the measure of the ways in which insurance companies and their agents conduct themselves in the marketplace. In other words, market conduct examines how companies and agents comply with state laws regulating (among other things):

- ✔ Sales, and marketing
- ✔ Underwriting and issuance of insurance products
- ✔ Policyholder service
- ✔ Complaint handling
- ✔ Claims handling
- ✔ Policy termination practices.

Market conduct regulation examines the treatment of insureds, applicants for insurance, and claimants, by insurance companies and their representatives. Proper market conduct means conducting insurance business fairly and responsibly.

In the past few years, a series of front-page scandals, million dollar lawsuits, and a tidal wave of regulatory attention have propelled market conduct to the forefront of insurance industry issues, at times even pushing financial solvency aside as the industry's top concern.

Market conduct reform is transforming the insurance industry; especially in life insurance, where sales and marketing methods are most easily abused. Responding to both huge lawsuits and regulatory pressure, companies are focusing on doing things by the book. Entire compliance departments have mushroomed where once a small staff of two or three would suffice.

Financial Fallout from Market Conduct Problems

A recent analysis of the life insurance industry's second year of disappointing sales results largely blames "fallout from market conduct problems ... as insurers struggled to regain public confidence."

The three leading life insurers in 1995, Metropolitan Life, Prudential, and New York Life, all suffered from negative publicity, lawsuits, and allegations of misleading sales practices. (*Best's Review, Life/Health* August 1996).

A.M. Best Company, an insurance company rating organization, announced in November 1995 that it will consider company market conduct compliance programs as an integral part of the rating process for life and health insurers. One of the "Big 6" accounting firms now includes market conduct issues as part of their audit process. These actions underline the extent to which market conduct problems can affect a company's financial and competitive position.

"Disruptions from market conduct problems that lead to lower distribution, productivity, lost sales opportunities, and weakened policy persistency will not only hurt current financial results but will have significant competitive implications over the longer term," said Michael L. Albanese, A.M. Best Company vice president, in announcing the change.

Regulators tend to agree, and often see a correlation between poor treatment of policyholders (mostly with regard to claims payment) and financial solvency problems.

A Catalog of Recent Crackdowns

The Metropolitan Life Insurance scandal which erupted in 1994 was the first large-scale example of the industry's latest image problem. MetLife and its agents were found to have utilized deceptive and misleading marketing practices to replace consumers' insurance policies or sell them new whole life policies. Regulators in Florida, Pennsylvania, and Texas investigated and filed complaints against MetLife agents and the company itself.

The regulators found that MetLife agents used misleading tactics to persuade consumers to replace existing policies; using the cash values from the existing policies to purchase new coverage for little or no additional premium (a process also known as **churning**). In many cases, once the value of the older policy was exhausted (usually after just a few years), the consumer would learn he or she was responsible for large and unexpected premium payments. The Pennsylvania Insurance Department, in summarizing its market conduct exam results, charged that a "principal motivating influence" was the "allure of high commissions realized by MetLife agents" for replacing coverage.

Also, it was found that the agents made unsupportable statements of future cash values, improperly sold life insurance disguised as "retirement" or "savings" plans, and incorrectly referred to premium payments as "deposits" without disclosing that the customer was purchasing insurance.

Fallout from the MetLife debacle has been widespread. Agents for the company were dismissed and/or had their licenses revoked; some in turn sued the company for wrongful discharge. The company was fined $1.5 million by the Pennsylvania Insurance Department, $1.2 million by the Texas Insurance Department, and $20 million in a multi-state settlement stemming from improper activities in the Tampa, Florida offices. MetLife was compelled to offer refunds or restitution to customers affected by the sales practices. Total payout in restitution and fines will reach an estimated $100 million. After MetLife's revenue from new business fell over 50%, A.M. Best dropped the company's rating from A++ to A+. (MetLife experienced better results in 1995 with sales up 17%).

The New York Life class action suit was precipitated by allegations of wrongdoing in conjunction with three common sales practices:

- ✔ Using policy values to pay new premiums due
- ✔ Selling insurance to meet retirement objectives, and
- ✔ Unnecessarily selling replacement coverage.

New York Life maintained that it engaged in no "systematic" wrongdoing, claimed its sales materials were and had always been in compliance with disclosure requirements, and blamed the problems on declining interest rates, lower industry earnings, changes in tax laws, and "isolated problems" with its representatives. However, the company acknowledged in the settlement language that "some policyholders may not have fully appreciated the significance" of the non-guaranteed elements of life insurance policy illustrations used at the time of sale.

In the settlement, the company offered policyholders either "class relief" in the form of options (premium loans, enhanced policies) intended to alleviate the impact of poorer-than-expected policy performance, or individual "alternative dispute resolution" available to policyowners who believed they could establish that misrepresentation occurred in the sales process.

In July 1996, a multi-state task force made up of 30 cooperating state insurance departments eclipsed MetLife's $20

Churning

Churning is the illegal practice of inducing an existing life insurance policyholder to use the cash value in the existing policy to purchase newer, higher face value, and more expensive life insurance policies with the same company. The selling agent earns a commission on the sale.

Widespread Abuses

"The abuses reviewed by the task force involved more than simply a few rogue agents or isolated instances of improper sales presentations. The abuses were widespread throughout all regions of the country," said New Jersey Insurance Commissioner Elizabeth Randall, who headed the task force. "Prudential failed to act responsibly concerning information available to it regarding both sales practices and agent misconduct, including misrepresentations and instances of forgery."

million fine with a $35 million fine against Prudential Insurance Company for deficiencies in marketing practices, internal systems, and agent training and discipline.

Policyholders claimed they were misled into using the built-up cash value of older life insurance policies to purchase newer, more expensive coverages. These "churning" practices were alleged to have occurred between 1982 and 1995. In some instances, agents arranged for the additional premiums on the new policies to be paid from the remaining value of the older policy without the knowledge or consent of the policyholder.

In addition to the fine, Prudential agreed to a remediation program which provides restitution to harmed policyholders through partial or even full premium refunds, continued coverage with no additional premiums due, and/or policy enhancements. The remediation program will be monitored by a regulatory oversight panel. A toll-free number has been set up to answer policyholder questions about the remediation process (1-800-736-8913). The restitution plan could cost Prudential more than $410 million.

The Pennsylvania Department of Insurance conducted its own, separate market conduct examination of Prudential's regional offices in Dresher, Pennsylvania, and in July 1996 levied a $1.5 million fine against the company "for deterrence and punishment of improper conduct".

"We focused our review on consumer complaints, advertising, forms filing and approval, and sales and marketing practices," said Dennis Shoop, director, bureau of enforcement.

Regulators are quick to point out that the practices uncovered in these investigations are not confined to MetLife, New York Life, or Prudential. A broader study of life insurance sales and marketing practices industry-wide will be undertaken by an NAIC working group, which then will develop guidelines and make recommendations for life insurance transactions.

Agents and Market Conduct

Agents provide advice and counsel in helping consumers understand one of the most complicated purchases they will ever make. As insurance products become more complex, there is more opportunity for consumers to be confused. Studies show that four out of five Americans feel their insurance policies are too difficult to understand, and most consumers do not understand what their policies cover.

Agents are expected to service a client's changing needs, and traditionally make a commission only when a sale is made. Therein lies the blessing and curse of agent services. While the agent ideally should be committed to serving the customer, he or she needs to make sales in order to make a living. Insurance companies, while trying to increase their focus on agent sales practices, still keep the pressure to sell high.

Agent activities aren't easily monitored. Much of the nation's insurance sales force works as independent agents, representing several insurance companies at a time, so insurance companies obviously have the most difficulty controlling what the agent says to the consumer "over the table".

Says one corporate compliance executive, "When the agent is alone in the room with the client, any oral comments made by the agent can leave us vulnerable. We can train them, but short of wiring them for sound we can't really control what they say."

"Of course companies are not capable of policing absolutely all agent activity," acknowledges Al Dawson, managing counsel of the American Council of Life Insurance (ACLI). "The best a company can do is have in place a reasonable program of supervision for monitoring, detection, and prevention. These will not ensure against all possible misconduct but certainly speak in favor a company's activities when and if both the regulators and the plaintiff attorneys arrive on the scene."

State Market Conduct Examinations

States regulate insurance by setting standards and monitoring competition in the marketplace. In the 1980s, after several large insurers became insolvent as a direct result of regulatory failure, the states' ability to soundly regulate the financial solvency of insurers came under heavy scrutiny, and much of the later 1980s was spent toughening financial solvency regulation. Lately, states have turned their attention from financial solvency to broader consumer protection through market surveillance and regulation.

Money Blurs the Interpretations

"Agents understand their responsibilities as well as they wish to understand them," says one former regulator. "Money tends to blur the interpretations for some agents. This can work to the detriment of the company or the insured party, depending upon the situation.

"For instance, finding that one customer who 'can't say no' can mean two things: either the agent will oversell policies to that person, or make a realization about the appropriateness of policies and refrain from doing so. The choice is his to make.

"Conversely, an agent can ignore the duties owed to an insurer, placing inappropriate risks with the company, advancing premiums on behalf of an insured, commingling funds, or committing other violations."

Heads in the Sand

"A lot of companies still have their heads in the sand on this issue," warns Kay Doughty, the former insurance commissioner for Massachusetts who now helps insurers prepare for market conduct exams. "I have yet to go into a company and not find a problem."

Market Conduct Examinations = Non-Financial Regulation

The non-financial regulatory activities of an insurance department fall under the broad heading of **market conduct**. A **market conduct examination** takes place when state insurance department investigators examine the business practices and operations of an insurer and its agents. During a market conduct examination, state examiners investigate the records and practices of an insurance company and determine whether the company is in fact in compliance with state laws, regulations, or orders of the insurance commissioner, as well as the company's own contract provisions.

For the most part, state examiners concentrate on an insurer's general business practices rather than random violations or isolated incidents of misconduct. Any pattern that seems to indicate that a violation is a "general business practice" will likely result in sanctions and penalties, as will evidence of "systematic wrongdoing" by a company. (In the New York Life class action lawsuit, the company maintained that there was no systematic wrongdoing by the company, and if any consumers were misled, it was because of isolated deceptive acts by individual agents.)

State insurance departments monitor agent activities in conjunction with market conduct regulation. A market conduct examination mostly surveys broad areas such as the insurer's:

- ✔ Certificate of authority
- ✔ Claims practices
- ✔ Advertising and marketing
- ✔ Forms and rates, and
- ✔ Underwriting guidelines

However, examiners will also review agent-related factors such as:

- ✔ Licensing
- ✔ Appointments
- ✔ Sales activities (including field underwriting, solicitation, disclosure, sales practices, and policy illustrations)

Types of Market Conduct Exams

Market conduct exams fall into several different categories.

- ✔ **Comprehensive** exams are full scope exams which examine every possible market conduct aspect of an insurer's operation: company operations/management, complaint handling, marketing and sales, licensing, policyholder service, underwriting, and claims handling. Some states require that these be performed at regular intervals as required by statute, either as part of a regular financial examination or separately.
- ✔ **Targeted** exams are specific to one or a few areas of concern. Targeted exams may be called without advance notice and are usually in response to a volume of consumer complaints.
- ✔ **Re-exams** are "follow up" exams conducted to determine whether a company has complied with recommendations or administrative orders from a previous market conduct exam.
- ✔ **Multi-state** exams (also referred to as "zone" exams) are exams in which multiple states participate in the review process.
- ✔ **Desk** exams are records inspections that occur off company premises and rely on the company to provide the necessary information.
- ✔ **Specialized** exams may include reviews of specialty insurers or regulated entities such as motor clubs, third-party administrators, multiple employer welfare associations, health maintenance organizations, etc.

Examiners may be insurance department employees or contract employees specially trained in conducting market conduct examinations for state departments of insurance.

The National Association of Insurance Commissioners (NAIC) produces a *Market Conduct Examiners Handbook* which provides guidelines for state examiners to follow when conducting market conduct examinations. In fact, the NAIC has recommended a "separate and distinct" program of market surveillance for the protection of policyholders since 1974.

IRES Certificate Programs for Examiners

The Insurance Regulatory Examiners Society (IRES) offers two certification programs; the "Accredited Insurance Examiner" (AIE) and the "Certified Insurance Examiner" (CIE).

The AIE is attained by completion of eight courses in either property/casualty or life/health. Once an individual has attained the AIE, he or she can earn the CIE designation by taking an additional four courses in the other field.

The Society's programs offer ongoing education, training, and career advancement, and encourage professionalism and integrity among state regulatory professionals, including investigators, policy analysts, rate analysts, complaint handlers, financial examiners, field examiners, department actuaries, and attorneys.

IRES
130 N. Cherry, Ste. 202
Olathe, KS 66061
(913) 768-4700

Among the company operations subject to review during a market conduct examination:

- ✔ Status of the company's Certificate of Authority and lines of authority
- ✔ Producer licensing, appointment, and termination practices
- ✔ Whether the company has a written compliance plan, an antifraud plan, and internal (or external) audit procedures
- ✔ Handling of premium notices, billing, unearned premiums, and refunds
- ✔ Handling of complaints about the company made directly to the company
- ✔ Handling of complaints about the company made to the insurance department
- ✔ Policy forms and endorsements (must be in accordance with insurer's rate and form filings)
- ✔ Marketing and solicitation
- ✔ Underwriting practices (including rejections and declinations) must not be unfairly discriminatory and must be applied consistently in accordance with the insurer's underwriting guidelines
- ✔ Agent sales practices
- ✔ Company oversight of general agents, managing general agents, and third-party administrators
- ✔ Communication of compliance issues with the field force, and producer training materials
- ✔ Producer compensation agreements
- ✔ Replacement practices (for life and health insurance)
- ✔ Cancellation and nonrenewal of policies (policy termination must be according to policy provisions and state law)
- ✔ Provisions on reinstatement, policy loans, nonforfeiture values, cash value, and interest (for life insurance)
- ✔ Proper handling of unearned premiums and refunds
- ✔ Rating (including making sure the policies issued conform to the insurer's rate and form filings)
- ✔ Claims handling (including accident reports, adjuster logs, correspondence and compliants, subrogation and salvage documentation)

- ✔ Policyholder service (including timely response to inquiries, applications, claims etc. and communications with policyholders)

Life/Health vs. Property/Casualty Exams

Life/health insurance carriers are considered especially good candidates for market conduct exams, particularly because there are certain ways life insurance is marketed that lend themselves to abuse. But clearly, deceptive sales tactics can be used in connection with any product and any distribution system. Property/casualty carriers are not exempt from problems in market conduct, particularly with regard to agent practices.

There are of course distinctions made when the company being examined is a life/health insurer or a property/casualty insurer. Examiners reviewing a life and health insurer will look at issues unique to those contracts, such as:

- ✔ Nonforfeitures
- ✔ Policy rescissions
- ✔ Reinstatement
- ✔ Replacement and conservation materials
- ✔ Lapsed policies
- ✔ Use of buyers guides, policy summaries, and disclosures
- ✔ Continuation of benefits
- ✔ Post claims underwriting

Examiners reviewing a property/casualty company would consider things like:

- ✔ Rating manuals and rate cards
- ✔ Classifications
- ✔ Payment plans
- ✔ Policy fees and discounts
- ✔ Subrogation practices

The Examination Process

Usually an insurance company receives about 60 days advance notice of an impending market conduct exam. The

Regulators Move to Private Industry

Transitioning from insurance department work to helping regulated companies with compliance issues is something of a trend.

Alaska's former insurance director, David Walsh, left office in January 1995 to oversee AIG's regulatory compliance and licensing divisions.

In April 1996, after nine years as Virginia's insurance commissioner, Steven Foster accepted a position as vice president of corporate compliance for Prudential.

Honest Efforts Pay Off

In helping one insurer preparing for a market conduct exam, former Massachusetts Commissioner Doughty discovered that the company had misread a change in the law and failed to file a rate (as required) for two years.

"We came clean, admitted 'here's what happened, here's how it happened, here's how we can avoid it in the future.'... If regulators see an honest effort to achieve compliance and fix problems, it makes a difference."

notice identifies the documents that will be needed, such as the company's annual statement, prior examination reports, etc., and may identify the areas of concern, who the examiner-in-charge will be, how many examiners there will be, and what their requirements for physical space and supplies will be. The exam typically will cover the last 12 months, but may extend back up to three years.

The Four C's

How an insurance company responds to the advance notice may set the tone for the entire examination. Regulators encourage the four C's:

- ✔ Compliance
- ✔ Cooperation
- ✔ Candor
- ✔ Consumer Protection

But Lew Melahn, former Director of the Missouri Department of Insurance, who now helps shepherd insurance companies through market conduct examinations, feels differently. "When a notice of examination arrives at an insurance company," he asserts, "it should be considered a declaration of war."

"It sometimes can be," agrees former Commissioner Doughty. "I try to give the company a 30,000 foot view of what to expect, and what to do next. There may be some quick fixes we can put in place before the DOI gets there, like making sure the complaint register is in order."

Prior to a market conduct exam the department of insurance (DOI) exam team usually:

- ✔ Familiarizes itself with the company's history of violations
- ✔ Reviews the results of past market conduct exams and
- ✔ Financial exams, and
- ✔ Identifies documents it will need to review such as the insurer's underwriting and claims manuals

The exam team has broad powers and may expand the scope of the exam beyond that addressed in the initial notice. For example, in conducting an examination of a life/health company, Colorado examiners initially planned to look at just the indemnity and managed care business. But in order to have access to a large enough sample, the examiners expanded the scope of the exam to include the comapny's HMO business, as well.

Exam Expense

The expense of a market conduct exam is most often borne by the insurance company being examined. This would include the cost of the examiner's salary, expenses, travel, lodging, and meals as well as providing any support staff, temporary office space, telephones, computers, office supplies, etc. made available to the examination team. The costs to the company may also include any penalties and administrative fines which may result from an exam, which can amount to hundreds of thousands of dollars.

Exit Conference

Upon completion of the onsite examination, the exam team will commonly hold a wrap-up or exit conference summarizing their findings and advising the company of the proper resolution procedures. The company is expected to implement changes and corrective measures where appropriate, and often a follow-up exam may be scheduled within 12-18 months to ensure the required changes have been made. The process is time consuming: market conduct exams can last anywhere from a few weeks to several months, and sometimes it can take more than a year to reach a stipulated agreement on the results of the exam. Once the final examination report is filed (sometimes as a public document, depending on the state), formal hearings may be needed, and the results may then be reported to the NAIC's Regulatory Information Retrieval System (RIRS) database (a centralized database of state regulatory and disciplinary information).

Administrative Action

When violations are found, administrative actions against the company can include:

- ✔ Requiring prompt corrective action (including refunds, correction of claims underpayments, etc.)
- ✔ Consent orders
- ✔ Imposing fines

Advice to Companies: Internal Team

One challenge faced by insurance companies is that not only are there differences between how different states conduct their exams, but enforcement styles within a state may differ from exam team to exam team.

In some instances, the examiner-in-charge may alert the company to what the exam focus will be, but it can be difficult for the company to tell in advance where the exam priorities and emphasis will lie.

Many times it is a good idea for the insurance company to schedule a pre-exam conference and assemble an internal team made up of one contact from each area of the company as well as a coordinator who is accessible to the exam team and meets with them on a daily basis.

Consumer Advocates Critical of State Performance

A 1995 report by the Center for Insurance Research, a consumer advocacy group, suggests that many states lack some of the "basic legal authorities necessary to fully protect consumers from market conduct abuses".

In conducting a comparative analysis of the Unfair Trade Practices and Unfair Claims Settlement Practices Acts of several states, the Center concluded that the laws themselves and the level to which they are enforced are insufficient for consumer protection.

The report is critical of performance guidelines proposed by the NAIC, stating "the proposed advisory guidelines are worse than nothing to the extent they project a false image that the states and the NAIC are taking market conduct seriously."

✔ Suspending or revoking the company's Certificate of Authority

One state regulator, speaking about imposing fines and penalties, said "$50,000 to $100,000 isn't going to hurt an insurance company ... if we really want to get someone's attention, we send out a press release."

But many regulators agree the amount of any fines imposed against the carrier depends on the severity of the violations and whether the violations seem to be honest mistakes or systemic problems. Colorado's Deputy Insurance Commissioner Maryellen Waggoner stresses that "The problems are pointed out to the company and the company is expected to make the appropriate changes."

The "Ultimate Consumer Protection"

Initially, market conduct exams were performed in conjunction with or as part of a regular financial solvency examination. But an increasing number of state insurance departments now perform examinations exclusively focusing on market conduct.

According to research by the NAIC, more than 1,400 market conduct exams were being conducted in 1994, an increase of 45% since 1990. As might be expected, some states are more active than others. In 1994, 13 states performed no exclusive market conduct exams, but Arizona conducted 230, Florida—225, Georgia—129, Maryland—103, Missouri—92, and Connecticut—86. (When you consider combined financial and market conduct exams, the numbers go up significantly.)

An average of 1,300 insurance companies are licensed to do business in each state, so regulators are inclined to focus their limited resources on their domestic insurers, and examine them roughly every three to five years. While some states aggressively regulate this area, according to the Insurance Regulatory Examiners Society (IRES), most states conduct fewer than 15 market conduct examinations per year.

Colorado's Maryellen Waggoner says the goal of market conduct exams is "not to levy fines, but to serve as the ultimate in consumer protection. The issues looked at are issues consumers are concerned with; things that directly affect policyholders."

Different State Approaches to Market Conduct

Most states will consider complaints about claims, underwriting, sales, advertising, and rating all as reasons for triggering a targeted market conduct exam. Illinois uses a market conduct annual statement that measures complaint ratios (number of complaints compared to premium volume) and then targets lines of insurance for exams. Having fewer routine scheduled exams allows the state to allocate resources to the companies that seem to need it most and address only the areas (like claims handling) that seem to be problem areas. As a result, most of Illinois' exams are triggered by consumer complaints stemming from claims handling.

Colorado regularly conducts targeted market conduct exams based on consumer complaints or other evidence of problems such as inconsistencies in the insurer's annual statement or failure to respond to inquiries. Agent issues are not the primary focus but are looked at in conjunction with other market conduct issues. A final report is written on site by the examiner. "There should be no surprises to the company at this tme," says Waggoner. "As the exam progresses there is lots of communication and plenty of opportunities to resolve questions and problems." Colorado also conducts "desk" exams, which consist of a request for documents to review. For example, in order to audit companies selling credit insurance, desk exams work because permissible loss ratio are specified by law. A check of company documents can easily establish compliance or noncompliance, reports Waggoner.

In Missouri, the examiner in charge meets with the company coordinator prior to the exam to provide guidance on what materials will be required (a list of agents, records of commissions paid, dates of agent appointments and terminations, etc.). Licensing, underwriting, and claims practices are reviewed together.

The Missouri Insurance Department publishes the results of its market conduct examinations in its *Public Policies* newsletter. The most common violations and penalties for agent-related activities in Missouri include:

- ✔ Failure to notify the department of insurance of "for cause" agent terminations
- ✔ Paying commissions to non-appointed agents
- ✔ Paying commissions to agencies without a current copy of their license on file
- ✔ Failure to have a copy of agents' and agencies' licenses on file
- ✔ Failure to notify the department of appointment and termination dates of agents
- ✔ Failure to maintain copies of agent appointments and terminations

- ✔ Accepting applications with forged agent's signature
- ✔ Failure to date stamp agencies' licenses

New York examines market conduct operations as part of the regular statutory "financial" examination of insurance companies. The results of market conduct exams in New York are often made public via press releases.

"Georgia tries to maintain a cycle of periodic market conduct examinations," says Martin Wilson, a former deputy insurance commissioner who now provides insurance counsel through the Atlanta law firm Troutman Sanders. "Targeted exams can take place at any time, and can be secured against a company, an agent, an agency, a third party administrator, or other entity under the jurisdiction of the commissioner. ... Most of the time, agent practices are only an incidental part of market conduct exams. However, if the actions of a particular agent have been the reason for a targeted exam, the examiners will take a look at the problems related to the conduct of that particular agent, then try to determine if the conduct can be generalized regarding other agents of the insurer. The objective is to determine whether there is a company-wide or company-taught practice, course of conduct, selling pattern, or other indication of pervasiveness."

California reported completing 53 market conduct exams in 1994, and recovered $324,372 for insureds and claimants. Common findings included problems with:

- ✔ Rescissions
- ✔ Total loss settlements
- ✔ Unfair claims settlements
- ✔ Unfair discrimination
- ✔ Failure to maintain adequate records
- ✔ Failure to provide good driver discounts to eligible applicants
- ✔ Failure to provide timely notice of nonrenewal
- ✔ Failure to provide dividend statements.

California's 1995 investigation into Allianz Life Insurance Company sales practices resulted in a $5.1 million settlement ($750,000 in fines, $1.75 million towards an

How the NAIC Tracks State Exams

The NAIC maintains computerized information systems to help facilitate the exchange of information between states.

Each state is encouraged (but not required) to share both exam schedulings and exam results through the Examination Tracking System (ETS).

The ETS can be used to provide reports for pre-exam analysis as well as follow-up reports to assist in historical and trend analysis.

underserved communities insurance program, and the remainder in restitution to policyholders).

Maryland's life and health market conduct unit reviews sales practices, advertising materials, underwriting practices, processing of claims, and nonforfeiture values. In 1993 the unit began examining agency records and practices as part of the market conduct exams; over 453 agent/agency investigations were completed, resulting in:

- ✔ 18 license revocations
- ✔ 6 license suspensions
- ✔ $19,900 in administrative penalties, and
- ✔ $51,768 in restitution.

Virginia conducts targeted exams, focusing on advertising practices, policy loans (making sure the rate of interest is that stated on the policy), and the flow of commission payments (any discrepancies will cause the investigator to follow up with agency records. Virginia also reviews policies and forms (to ensure they are DOI approved), cancellation and nonrenewal practices, and any changes which have taken place at the company since the last examination. If regulatory action is necessary, there is a $1,000 minimum and maximum $5,000 penalty per violation. If a cease and desist order has been violated, the penalty goes to $10,000 per violation.

Delaware evaluates the company's ability to self-evaluate, monitor, and correct problems. The maximum penalty is $50,000 per violation, reports Delaware's Gene Reed, "But it could be as little as $1 if the company signs a consent order." Delaware has also been known to randomly visit insurance agencies throughout the state and go through their books.

The Trend toward Multi-State Market Conduct Exams

Virtually all states perform some type of market conduct examination procedure; about 42 states engage in specific market conduct reviews on a targeted or routine basis. Only about 30 states have formal market conduct exams, the others find out about market conduct problems through the "treatment of policyholders" portion of regular financial examinations.

But shrinking state regulatory budgets combined with an ever-increasing workload demand a more efficient approach

Protecting Policyholders

"If policyholders have been harmed, you want to get to the bottom of it quickly, and you want to be able to decide on the appropriate remediation for the policyholders." says Paul DeAngelo, director of enforcement and consumer Protection for the New Jersey Department of Insurance.

"The advantage of conducting multi-state market conduct exams is you can build on what other states have done. If other states have looked at a company's advertising and it's clean, chances are it's clean and you can concentrate on other areas."

than sequential exams by different state departments of insurance.

"While the responsibility of the insurance department to protect policyholders and claimants is paramount, we need to make every attempt to fulfill that responsibility as efficiently as possible," wrote Gene Reed, director of licensing for the Delaware Insurance Department, in a letter to the National Association of Insurance Commissioners.

Former commissioner Doughty admits that during her tenure Massachusetts didn't perform any market conduct examinations. "We had all we could do to conduct the required financial examinations of domestic insurers," she says.

To make matters worse, the companies are just as pressed for resources as the states. An insurance company that does business in all 50 states is responsible for complying with 50 different sets of insurance statutes and regulations.

"Companies are unduly burdened by having several states at once involved in market conduct examinations," says Doughty. "We are seeing more mergers, acquisitions, and consolidations among insurance companies. The people who are left after downsizing are being asked to oversee more areas and take on more responsibilities, and compliance issues can too easily fall through the cracks."

Wade Harrell of Liberty Mutual Insurance Company, writing in *The Regulator* newsletter, described "1994 when our front doors were revolving quite rapidly to accommodate multiple states' examination needs." Liberty Mutual began 1994 with 16 examinations underway, closed 10, and new examinations were called by 10 states. The company thus began 1995 just as it had 1994, with 16 examinations at various stages of completion.

Multi-state market conduct exams are increasingly being considered a realistic solution. Some market conduct exams uncover industry-wide problems, which transcend the practices of any one company. States are interested in learning whether other states are detecting the same problems. Companies have long complained about the lack of coordination between states conducting market conduct examinations; several different states may be reviewing a particular company at a time. It seems likely companies would find a single, multi-state investigation much easier to accommodate than many separate state investigations.

"We need to develop market conduct procedures that are geared towards evaluating the overall performance of companies in the specific business areas, not specific states," says Delaware's Reed. "If we can develop a zone examination process that coordinates the efforts of the states into a single examination that meets the department's needs, then regulation will function more effectively for everyone involved."

In 1995, the New Jersey Department of Insurance led a multi-state examination into allegations of improper sales and marketing activities at The Prudential. The task force's stated purpose was to determine the scope and seriousness of improper sales activity, to correct any harm to policyholders resulting from improper sales practices, to develop appropriate remedies and regulations to prevent such practices in the future, and to ensure the public can continue to have confidence in their purchase of life insurance. Thirty state insurance departments cooperated with the examination, which resulted in a 232-page summary report, a remediation program to correct harm done to policyholders, and the largest fine ever levied against a U.S. insurer: $35 million.

How Multi-State Exams Work

States participating in a multi-state market conduct exam may be identified as the:

- ✔ **discovery state** that initiates the examination,
- ✔ **lead state** that directs the examination, and/or
- ✔ **domicile state** where the insurance company is domiciled

Multi-state examinations may have both active and passive participants; **active** participants send examiners to conduct the analysis; **passive** participants are kept informed of the results and resulting punitive actions, if any. In the Prudential task force investigation, there were 12 active and 18 passive participants.

The result of a multi-state examination is a **core report** or **audit summary**, which consists mainly of statistical data on topics like replacement etc., but does not cite specific violations of state law. Participating states then develop specific addenda to the core report, citing specific law violations (if any), adopt it as the official state report, and use it to generate corrective action or sanctions as appropriate.

Former commissioner Doughty is enthusiastic about the potential for multi-state examinations, especially "if they can be made more uniform. The NAIC committees have had great success with creating uniformity in financial examinations," she says. "And the new (NAIC) *Market Conduct Examiners Handbook* goes a long way toward raising the level of professionalism of market conduct exams, detailing the criteria against which companies should be measured." In fact, the

Patterns of Misconduct Drive Class Actions

"To the extent that patterns of agent misconduct emerge and a company takes no action with respect to them, then you have the makings of a major lawsuit on a count of improper supervision or failure to adequately monitor, and a violation of the Unfair Trade Practices Acts," says one industry expert. "These of course are what have been driving some of the recent class action litigation involving some of the very large companies."

Attorneys Fishing for Torts

Richard D. Rogers, deputy director of the consumer market division at the Illinois Department of Insurance (and one of the country's leading experts in market conduct regulation), reports a steadily increasing volume of requests from attorneys for information regarding market conduct violations and subsequent penalties.

Attorneys on a "fishing expedition" will call the insurance department to find out what types of violations are being uncovered, reports Rogers, and then will contact policyholders affected by the violation in order to consolidate a punitive/bad faith tort action against the insurance company.

While regulators might not be favorably inclined (or even have the staff, time or resources) to release such information, they must respond to Freedom of Information Act requests.

NAIC has recently adopted at the committee level a formal procedure for the conduct of multi-state examinations.

Problems with Multi-State Exams

Not everyone is enthusiastic about multi-state exams. While they may seem like a good idea, they are difficult in practice because of state-to-state differences. "The number one problem is that there are 50 sovereign states," says a compliance expert from USF&G. "The exam report may be uniform but the states' responses to the report are unique."

Liberty Mutual's Harrell senses that "the regulatory community is far from 100% supportive of the implementation of multi-state examinations ... I believe the regulated community is more positive about the concept of multi-state market conduct examinations than are the regulators."

Pennsylvania Insurance Commissioner Linda Kaiser recommends a return to the single-state exam process, citing concerns about the appropriateness of multi-state exams for property/casualty companies and the "piling on" effect of states attaching to a multi-state exam without sending their own examining team.

Former Virginia deputy commissioner and long-time market conduct veteran, Pete Synnott, doubts that regulatory efficiency is achieved by multi-state exams. "A market conduct exam by three states results in three times the disruption in one third the time," says Synnott.

"Because the core of company activities to be examined by any state in a market conduct exam varies only slightly, a multi-state exam should be the norm," says former Georgia deputy commissioner Wilson. "But there really are very few effective multi-state market conduct exams being conducted at present. While they may be beneficial for examiners, it certainly can become a major expense for insurers."

There are also problems with subjectivity and differences in state priorities, philosophies, enforcement styles, differing requirements to public availability of information, differing due process requirements, and differences regarding how to handle proprietary information collected during exams. And these problems are compounded by states that use market conduct exams for political purposes and publicity, or that rely on market conduct fines and penalties for revenue generation.

The Class Action Monster

While a market conduct examination undertaken by a state insurance department could result in fines, penalties and negative publicity, there now looms the larger threat of class action lawsuits against a company through allegations of complicity with widespread deceptive practices.

Insurers are facing an increasing number of consumer "class action" lawsuits alleging misleading sales tactics and other abuses. The MetLife and New York Life cases served as an introduction to life insurance for the nation's plaintiff attorneys, who previously didn't seem to understand how to access the insurance industry.

Where are these lawsuits originating? In a trend that has proven particularly troubling to insurance companies and state insurance regulators alike, market conduct exam results are being "mined" by plaintiff attorneys to generate class action lawsuits.

Policyholders (or, more accurately, attorneys representing policyholders) who have allegedly been "wronged" by deceptive sales practices or other violations are using market conduct fines and penalties as the basis for punitive damages and bad faith tort actions against insurance companies.

Exportable Actions

An important question is whether market conduct violations are "exportable" actions. Market conduct exam results are matters of public record (and will become even more widely distributed once the industry's electronic information networks become operational). But most state laws are silent on whether private causes of action can arise from violations of the Unfair Trade Practices Acts. And regulators have few guidelines or constraints regarding the release of market conduct information.

"A market conduct exam conducted by the state is an 'official exercise' and there is probably a point in time at which the results are discoverable. I don't think there's anything to prevent an aggressive plaintiff attorney from getting whatever information that attorney wants to get," says ACLI's Dawson. "But litigators do not depend entirely on market conduct exams, they get information from lots of sources: the *Wall Street Journal*, the trade press, complaint records, agents, and consumers."

Cases of Questionable Merit

ACLI's managing counsel Al Dawson notes that as a legal remedy, class actions have a "certain value in achieving efficient and economic results for consumers or classes similarly situated.

"Unfortunately, in recent times we believe the impetus of class actions has been more to the benefit of attorneys pursuing the cases rather than to the ultimate intended beneficiaries."

"We are also concerned with what appears to be an emerging tendency to fashion class action suits for the express intention of driving companies toward settlements in cases which may be of questionable merit but which would involve companies in otherwise extraordinary expense in conducting full defense."

Industry Organizations & Phone Numbers

American Council of Life Insurance
ACLI
(202) 624-2411

♦

American Institute for Chartered Property/Casualty Underwriters
AICPCU
(610) 644-2100

♦

Independent Insurance Agents Association
IIAA
(703) 683-4422

♦

Life Insurance Market Research Association
LIMRA
(800) 235-4672

♦

Life Underwriter Training Council
LUTC
(301) 913-5882

♦

National Association of Life Underwriters
NALU
(202) 331-6086

The class action trend continues. More lawsuits seeking class action status were filed in July 1995 against the Equitable Life of Iowa, New York Life, John Hancock Mutual Life, Equitable Life Assurance Society, and Equitable of Colorado alleging "vanishing premium" fraud. Understandably, companies are terrified by the prospect of time-consuming and expensive class action lawsuits stemming from market conduct examination results, not to mention the attendant bad publicity, lost sales, and damage to the industry's credibility.

Confidentiality Issues

"The confidentiality of market conduct reports may be the only answer," says Georgia's Wilson. "However, remember that most states do not allow a private cause of action; it is up to the commissioner, not the citizenry, to enforce the insurance code. Any company that does not have assurances that the insurance laws do not convey a right to go to court, as in a class action, probably has no real protections."

Texas Attorney General Dan Morales recently issued a formal opinion statement preserving the confidentiality of audit and work papers gathered during a Texas Department of Insurance examination into an insurer's financial condition or market conduct compliance. Ironically, this opinion statement preserving confidentiality replaces an earlier opinion that had taken a contrary view.

Industry Organizations Respond

To their credit, industry organizations have mustered a solid response to recent market conduct challenges, developing initiatives designed to teach ethical behavior and help restore consumer confidence. Since those engaged in the sale of insurance have long been regarded as professional advisors, agent groups such as the National Association of Life Underwriters, Independent Insurance Agents of America, Professional Insurance Agents, etc. have always had published "Codes of Ethics" subscribed to by their membership. Lately, these organizations have gone even further to advocate ethical conduct in the insurance industry.

The National Association of Life Underwriters (NALU) pioneered reform in policy illustrations by forming a Market Conduct Task Force in 1993, and has a Replacement Task Force looking into guidelines for reform and enforcement. "These problems will only continue to fester unless remedial steps are taken," says NALU immediate past president Allan G. Hancock. Market conduct has also been a main topic at recent NALU annual conventions, and is a regular feature in the *Life Association News* magazine and many other association publications.

The NALU and the Life Underwriter Training Council (LUTC), have revised course requirements for the LUTC Fellow (LUTCF) designation, which they jointly sponsor. Candidates must now complete the course *Piecing Together the Ethical Puzzle* in order to qualify for the LUTCF designation. The course deals with compliance, personal and professional ethics, proper business practices, and ethical issues and guidelines.

The American Council of Life Insurance (ACLI) established a CEO Task Force on Market Conduct in March 1994, "to promote collective performance improvement throughout the life insurance industry and strengthen consumer confidence." This task force produced a proposal, "Principles and Code of Ethical Market Conduct" establishing standards for ethical conduct, based on a set of six principles, to be voluntarily adopted by life insurers. A questionnaire was designed to help insurers assess their compliance.

Completion of both self and independent assessment would qualify a company to participate in an independent Market Conduct Organization, to be established as an independent subsidiary of the ACLI. Field tests of the proposal (which has received the endorsement of the National Association of Life Underwriters) were well received and the ACLI's Board has given its overwhelming acceptance to the proposal.

Many member companies have already indicated they will undergo the self assessment process as well as the third party assessment required by the program, reports ACLI's Dawson. Questions remain as to whether or not the program is appropriate to every size and type of company, says Dawson, so the program is being adapted and customized to make it as responsive as possible to the broadest range of member companies.

ACLI established a "Compliance Section" in September 1994 to identify and consider topics of significance to member company compliance officers, life insurance consumers, and regulators. The Compliance Section facilitates the exchange and dissemination of information and ideas on member company compliance policies, practices, and procedures. "It provides a forum for the compliance officers of member companies to meet, share experiences, and come up with solutions to problems in the marketplace," adds Dawson. The Section has enjoyed large, well-attended meetings consisting of a two-and-a-half day program of presentations, workshops, and papers. Also, ACLI has produced a *Guide to Market Conduct* for its member life companies which summarizes state market conduct requirements.

The American Institute for Chartered Property/Casualty Underwriters unveiled a new "Institute for Applied Ethics" in early 1995. Its goals are to identify and fund practical research in order to heighten awareness of ethical standards. The institute will fund studies into the ethical implications of business decisions made in the insurance industry, fund educational workshops on ethics, and provide speakers and moderators for ethics-related insurance functions. In March 1996, the organization sponsored five ethics symposiums to mark "Ethics Awareness Month."

Also, the American Institute's Code of Professional Ethics was recently revised to allow the Institute to deal with CPCUs who commit ethical breaches that result in serious crimes. Two new disciplinary rules provide for the loss of the CPCU designation and suspension from CPCU program participation for members who are convicted of crimes violating the society's rules of professional conduct.

LIMRA International (the Life Insurance Market Research Association) has several publications available for agents to help educate them with regard to ethical and market conduct issues, including *Selling Ethically: How Do I Benefit, The Trusted Advisor,* and *Are You in Compliance?*. Compliance issues are also frequently discussed in LIMRA's and as well as other insurance trade newsletters and magazines.

Contributions from the country's leading life and health insurers and associations helped establish The Life and Health Insurance Foundation for Education (LIFE) in 1994. The purpose of the foundation is to educate the public about the role and value of life and health insurance in society; why life and health insurance is critical, how it provides protection, and the value added by the services of professional agents. LIFE has initiated an advertising and consumer education campaign to improve the public's understanding and perception of the insurance industry which is expected to continue for at least the next three years. LIFE plans also to:

- ✔ Establish an interactive web site
- ✔ Conduct educational programs for high school students on insurance, and
- ✔ Sponsor seminars to educate journalists on insurance issues.

Also, LIFE and Newsweek Inc. have in conjunction launched a national contest to find and publicize the best "real life" stories from life insurance agents across the country.

Regulatory Response

The National Association of Insurance Commissioners is revising its *Market Conduct Examiners Handbook*, helping to set standards for examinations and guidelines for coordinated multi-state market conduct exams, and focusing on market conduct issues in the development of model laws such as the life disclosure and policy illustrations model law. The NAIC also worked with the Actuarial Standards Board to develop standards that will help actuaries consistently represent illustration assumptions.

However, unlike financial issues, which tend to be uniform from state to state, market issues are mainly local. So NAIC recommendations for overseeing market conduct must take into account state differences in regulatory philosophy. Also, while the model regulations developed at the NAIC are intended to encourage states to have the same minimum standards for regulatory efficiency, the model acts often are modified by the state's legislative process and may be lacking major components when finally adopted.

The regulatory response to the spotlight on market conduct has been activity in various NAIC committees as well as a flurry of state laws and regulations on subjects such as:

- ✔ Life disclosure
- ✔ Redlining
- ✔ Fair underwriting
- ✔ Policy illustrations
- ✔ Policy cancellations and nonrenewals
- ✔ Suitability and
- ✔ Complaint handling

For example, Florida adopted an anti-churning rule, effective in February 1996, which requires companies to adopt anti-churning procedures and disclose to prospects exactly how the premiums of a new or replacement policy would be paid.

New York regulators are working on disclosure laws that require agents to explain to customers how replacing an older policy with a new one is in their best interest. Pennsylvania has a reform proposal that will:

- ✔ Regulate the use of policy illustrations
- ✔ Eliminate incentives for churning
- ✔ Require insurers to track agents' replacement transactions and
- ✔ Increase civil penalties for misrepresentation

✔ Check Your Understanding

1. Identify the major areas of insurance company operations that are reviewed during a typical market conduct examination.

2. Which areas of the above are relevant to agent activities?

3. Describe the advantages and disadvantages of a multi-state market conduct exam.

CHAPTER 2

THE AGENT'S RESPONSIBILITIES TO POLICYHOLDERS

The insurance agent is key to the sale, marketing, underwriting, and delivery of insurance policies. Insurance agents and brokers remain the principal contacts for insurance consumers, and are expected to fulfill certain legal, professional, and ethical obligations toward their clients.

As a marketing representative of the insurer, it is the agent's responsibility to represent and market the insurer's products in an ethical and professional manner. This requires knowledge of various insurance products, learning about the prospect's insurance needs and problems, and the ability to solve these needs with the proper insurance products. Agents can be a valuable resource, providing helpful guidance on the most appropriate use of a family's assets and allowing them to achieve financial goals such as risk management, retirement planning, death protection, health care, asset protection, etc.

Above all, agents are expected to follow the Golden Rule of insurance sales: in spite of the headlines, in light of contractual restrictions, and within the confines of state and federal law, **always** do what is right for the customer.

Intrinsic Conflict of Interest

Yet there is a conflict of interest intrinsic to the agent-consumer transaction. While agents *should* make recommendations based on the client's needs, they need to sell policies in order to earn commissions and make a living. The pressure to sell emanates from the agent's own personal financial situation and of course, the agent's company and manager. The insurer may say it wants the field force to provide a careful needs analysis but, in fact, the reward system for the agents is based on sales — not service. If an agent discovers that less service and needs analysis can result in quicker sales, then the agent faces the ethical conflict of whether to make more sales and more money at the expense of the clients' needs.

The commission structure of most companies can also place the agent in the ethical dilemma of selling the "higher commission" products in lieu of those policies which may better serve the client's needs. For example, whole life with a higher commission may be sold in smaller amounts because of the higher premium at the expense of the client's need for larger quantities of insurance which could be provided by lower commission term insurance. Another ethical problem can arise because agents are compensated by commissions which are only earned if an applicant is approved for the insurance and a policy is issued. The agent may be persuaded to omit material information from the application or simply not tell the truth so that the policy will be approved.

Agents Not the Root Cause of All Evil

"Agents are quite sensitive to being characterized as the root cause of all the recent problems — and they're probably right," says Al Dawson, ACLI's managing counsel. "It's not fair or right to attribute all of the ills that have happened in the last several years to agents alone. Some of it had to do with the reward system, some of it had to do with inadequate training, some of it had to do with improper supervision by company management, a more permissive approach to how sales were being made, the result of 'unbundling' of products ... there were a lot of factors."

Regulating Agent Activities

State insurance departments consider the activities of licensed agents and brokers to be an increasingly important part of the market conduct regulation and examination process (although most regulators would like to say that the scrutiny of agent activities has been present all along).

States have passed a number of laws outlining agent responsibilities in the areas of fiduciary duty, licensing and continuing education, unfair trade practices, policy delivery, policy illustrations, replacement, disclosure, etc. Court decisions help refine the standards to which agents and brokers are held.

Clearly, the interchange between the insurance agent and the client has always been the most difficult to regulate. Complicating the problem is that much of the nation's insurance sales force works as independent agents, representing several insurance companies at a time.

Enforcement actions indicate that the insurance company owns any policy it issues regardless of the method of sale. And from recent class action lawsuits, clearly insurance companies also "own" any problems arising out of these policies.

This chapter describes the legal responsibilities established by an agent's relationship with the insurance company in regards to the policyholder, summarizes the agent's duties to the policyholder as outlined by state laws and industry practice, and explores what happens when the rules get broken.

Of course, some responsibility falls to the consumer, as well, to seek out alternate sources of information, make appropriate inquiries, shop a few different agents or companies before making a purchase, and not blindly trust the advice of a single agent. Nothing beats a well-informed consumer who understands the results of his or her purchasing decisions.

Agency Law Principles

An understanding of the law of agency is important because an insurance company, like many other companies, most often acts through agents. **Agency** is a relationship in which one person is authorized to represent and act for another person or for a corporation. An **agent** is a person authorized to act on behalf of another person, who is called the **principal**.

In insurance, the principal is the insurance company and the producer is the agent. Once empowered to act as an agent for a principal, the agent is legally assumed to **be** the principal in matters covered by the grant of agency:

- ✔ Contracts made by the agent are the contracts of the principal.
- ✔ Payment to the agent, within the scope of his or her authority, is payment to the principal.
- ✔ The knowledge of the agent is assumed to be the knowledge of the principal.

When one is empowered to act as an agent for a principal, he or she is legally assumed to be the principal in matters covered by the grant of agency.

Presumption of Agency

Agents are empowered to act on behalf of the insurance company in transacting insurance business with consumers. This empowerment (in the form of express, implied, and apparent authority) has gotten many agents and companies in trouble, especially when agents act beyond the scope of their authority, usually without the permission or knowledge of the insurance company.

If a company supplies an individual with forms and other materials (known as signs and evidences of authority) that make it appear that he or she is an agent of the company, a court will likely hold that a presumption of agency exists. The company is then bound by the acts of this individual whether or not he or she has been given this authority. The authority of an agent is of three types: express, implied or apparent.

Express Authority

Express authority is an explicit, definite agreement. It is the authority the principal gives the agent as set forth in his or her contract. The typical agency agreement gives the agent express authority to:

- ✔ Solicit applications for insurance
- ✔ Issue policies
- ✔ Collect premiums
- ✔ Cancel policies
- ✔ Retain a commission from the premiums collected

It is very important for an agent to know the limitations of the contract and to operate within its limits. To do otherwise could place the agent in a position of personal liability. An agent's actions and knowledge are binding on the insurance company, so the agent must be alert to the consequences of his or her actions and words.

Implied Authority

Implied authority is not expressly granted under an agency contract, but it is actual authority which the agent has to transact the principal's business in accordance with general business practices.

For example, if an agent's contract does not give him or her the express authority of collecting and submitting premium, but the agent does so on a regular basis, and the company accepts the premium, then the agent is considered to have implied authority. That is, it is a general business practice to collect premium, and by accepting the premium from the agent, the company has implied that the agent has the authority to conduct this practice.

Lingering Implied Authority

Lingering implied authority means that the agent carries "signs or evidences of authority." By having these evidences of authority an agent who is no longer under contract to an insurer could mislead applicants or insureds. When the agency relationship between agent and company has been terminated, the company will try, or should try, to get back all the materials it supplied to the former agent, including sales materials.

On the other hand, the public cannot assume that an individual is an agent merely because he or she says so. The agent must carry the credentials (for example the agent's license and appointment) and company documents (such as applications and rate books) that represent him or her as being an agent for an insurance company.

Apparent Authority

Apparent authority is the authority the agent seems to have because of certain actions undertaken on his or her part. This action may mislead applicants or insureds, causing them to believe the agent has authority which he or she does not, in fact, have. The principal may add to this assumption by acting in a manner that reinforces the impression of authority. For instance, an agent's contract usually does not grant the authority to reinstate a lapsed policy by accepting past due premiums. If, in the past, the company has allowed the agent to accept late premiums for that purpose, a court would probably hold that the policyowner had the right to assume that the agent's acceptance of premium was within the scope of his or her "apparent" authority.

Types of Agents

Companies that use agents to sell their products vary by whether the agents are employees or independent sales representatives.

Independent Insurance Agents

Independent insurance agents sell the insurance products of several companies and work for themselves or other agents. They sell their clients the policy that fits their needs best among the many insurers they represent, and are paid a commission for each sale. The independent agent owns the expirations of the policies he or she sells, meaning that that agent may place that business with another insurer upon renewal if in the best interest of the client.

Exclusive or Captive Agents

Exclusive or **captive agents** represent only one company. These agents are sometimes referred to as career agents working from career agencies. Most often, these captive or career agents are compensated by commissions. A career agent's compensation will normally consist of first year commissions and renewal commissions in subsequent years. First year commissions may represent 50% or more of a first year life insurance premium. Thereafter the renewal commissions will usually be 10% or less each year.

New agents may also be paid a training allowance for several months which serves as a salary for a limited period of time during which the new agent is being trained. Most companies will require that the career agent validate this training allowance by producing a certain amount of new business each month.

General Agents and Managing General Agents

If an agent hires, trains and supervises other career agents within a specific geographical area, he or she is referred to as a **general agent** or **managing**

general agent (MGA). The MGA is compensated by commissions earned on business he or she sells as well as an overriding commission (overrides) on the business produced by the other agents managed by the general agent. An MGA may receive additional compensation for administrative and service functions performed for policyholders, to help cover some of the agency's overhead expenses.

Lines of Insurance

Insurance agents, brokers, and solicitors (also known as producers in some states) are not only categorized by their function in the industry, but also by the line(s) of insurance they are licensed to sell.

Life and Health Agents

Life and health agents represent the insurer to the buyer with respect to the sale of life and health insurance products. The agents are appointed by the insurer and usually the agent's authority to represent the insurer is specified in the agency agreement between them. Life and health insurance agents generally do not have the authority to issue or modify insurance contracts, but are authorized to solicit, receive, and forward applications for the contracts written by their companies.

The agent may collect the first premium due with the application, but usually not subsequent premiums (except in industrial life insurance). The insurance company approves and issues the contract after receiving the application and premium from the applicant through the agent. The agent **cannot bind** coverage. This means that a life and health agent cannot commit to providing insurance coverage on behalf of the insurance company.

Property and Casualty Agents

Property and casualty agents are appointed by property and liability insurance companies, and generally have more authority. These agents **may bind** or commit their companies by oral or written agreement. A binder is a temporary contract, usually providing coverage for a short period of time (commonly 15 to 30 days, depending on the state). Binders may be used to provide written evidence of coverage before a policy has been received, or to provide temporary coverage pending the issuance of a policy. Coverage under a binder usually ends when coverage begins under a policy. To avoid any dispute, the agent who gives an oral binder should immediately record the effective date of coverage, the terms of coverage, and the names of the parties (insurer and insured). Property/casualty agents also sometimes inspect risks for the insurance company and collect premiums due, and may be authorized to issue many types of insurance contracts from their own offices.

While life insurers have historically been the most obvious target for agent-related market conduct review, examiners also scrutinize the relationship between property/casualty agents and their policyholders. For example, the NAIC *Market Conduct Examiners Handbook* recommends "particular emphasis" in reviewing dealings between managing general agents and policyholders, and being certain the company is adequately monitoring the MGA's activities. This involves not only reviewing MGA contracts but also MGA audit reports to ensure compliance with applicable statutes, rules, and regulations. The MGA contract should specify the responsibilities of the MGA with regard to recordkeeping and the responsibilities of the company for conducting audits of MGA activity.

Brokers, Solicitors, and Consultants

In contrast to the agent-client relationship in which the agent represents the insurer to the purchaser, a **broker** represents the buyer to the insurer. A broker may do business with several different insurers. Brokers are independent sales representatives who select insurance coverages from these various companies for their clients.

Brokers must be licensed just like agents and generally their routine activities and functions are similar to that of agents. Brokers solicit applications for insurance, may collect the initial premium, and deliver policies. In general, brokers do not have the authority to bind coverages.

A **solicitor** is a salesperson who works for an agent or a broker, most commonly in the property and casualty insurance field. Depending on the state, the solicitor may be required to obtain an agent's or broker's license, or may hold a special solicitor's license. Solicitors normally have a working agreement with an agent or broker specifying that the solicitor's primary functions are to solicit insurance, collect initial premiums and deliver policies. Solicitors cannot bind coverage.

A relatively small group of insurance professionals call themselves **insurance consultants**. Consultants are not paid by commission for the sales of insurance policies. Instead, they work strictly for the benefit of insureds and are paid a fee by the insureds they represent. In many states, insurance consultants hold a separate license.

Licensing Requirements

It seems hardly necessary to mention that one of an agent's most important responsibilities is to be legally and properly authorized to sell the insurance products he or she is selling. This means not only obtaining and maintaining as current the required license for the lines of insurance being sold, in all of the states in which the agent does business, but also possessing the knowledge and expertise to sell those lines of insurance, holding the proper appointments, and meeting all other legal requirements such as nonresident licensing, countersignature, bonding, placing surplus lines business, etc., as set out in state law.

Likewise, any agency employees that solicit insurance business will probably need to be licensed, as well, in accordance with state law. Practically speaking, this usually includes anyone who:

- ✔ Takes applications for insurance
- ✔ Receives or delivers insurance policies for a company
- ✔ Examines or inspects risks
- ✔ Receives, collects, or transmits insurance premiums

Agency employees who are regularly salaried clerical and administrative employees are usually not required to obtain an insurance license.

Failure to hold the appropriate license or appointment, and selling coverages without proper authority are among the most common agent-related violations cited during market conduct examinations. The DOI will instantly note if an agent was not appointed at the time of sale, and will not hesitate to sanction both the agent and the company.

Technical & Market Expertise

Agents provide advice to consumers during one of the most complicated purchases they will ever make. Insurance products have become more and more complex, so there is ample opportunity for consumers to be confused. Studies show that most consumers lack a clear understanding of how insurance works, and commonly do not understand what is covered by their own policies. Only a handful of people actually read the policy or even the sales literature provided with the policy.

A competent, educated agent can, in turn educate the public about insurance and help consumers make informed buying decisions about insurance. To do so, the agent must be knowledgeable about a broad spectrum of insurance products and should be able to explain the advantages and disadvantages of different types of policies, costs and terms, provisions, coverages, exclusions, limitations, etc. It is the mark of a poor agent to conduct a fact-finding analysis and then consistently recommend the same policy solution to every client. Unscrupulous agents use the consumer's lack of knowledge to sell inappropriate coverages.

Agents who are committed to keeping current with industry developments are in the best place to serve their clients well (and are in the best place to survive increased competition such as that from the financial services industry). The insurance industry is blessed with many opportunities for education and advancement, even college-level programs. Pursuing continuing education, joining and participating in industry associations, achieving professional designations such as the CLU and CPCU, are all excellent ways for an agent to demonstrate commitment to clients and to the profession.

Arguments have been made on whether being an insurance agent actually qualifies as a "profession". In his book *On Professions, Professionals, and Professional Ethics*, Ronald C. Horn, PhD, CPCU, CLU, summarizes the characteristics of a profession as follows:

- ✔ A commitment to high ethical standards
- ✔ A prevailing attitude of altruism
- ✔ Mandatory educational preparation and training
- ✔ Mandatory continuing education
- ✔ A formal association or society
- ✔ Independence
- ✔ Public recognition as a profession

Measured against these desirable characteristics of a profession, and depending on whether an agent is licensed in a state with educational requirements, the status of insurance agents as "professionals" is clearly debatable. Still, most agents would consider themselves as professionals, individuals with a certain level of competence, part of an occupational group engaged in a specific and identifiable career.

Client Servicing/Needs-Based Analysis

Needs-based selling and ongoing client service are among an agent's primary responsibility to the customer. A needs-based analysis is the only way to ensure that the customer gets the insurance product that is most appropriate to his or her goals and needs.

Today's insurance consumers tend to be more sophisticated with regard to personal finance and investments, and also more cynical. (Prospects may ask "Does this policy contain any accounting assumptions that might artificially inflate its cash value?")

Successful agents have dropped their hard sell orientation and have become market-driven with a strong customer orientation. The agent's function is to inform and educate the client about the insurance industry and insurance products.

Agents should give the client sufficient information about how the insurance product being recommended meets the client's specific needs, and should

Determining Suitability

A 32-year old woman receives a direct mail solicitation for long term care insurance. The policy is non-cancellable, guaranteed renewable for life and has an annual premium of $25. She calls her agent and asks whether this would be a suitable purchase.

What should her agent recommend? Will she need long term care insurance? Probably. Does she need it now? Probably not. But depending on her risk tolerance and desire for long-range planning, she may want to purchase this policy just to "lock in" the $25 per year rate.

A senior citizen walks into an insurance agency with a $250,000 cashier's check and asks to buy an annuity. Is this a suitable purchase? The agent first needs to find out a lot more information about the client. Is this all the money this person has in the world? If so, it would be unwise to sink it all into an annuity. When does the person want the annuity payments to begin? Is the goal to have the highest possible income from the annuity or would the person like to leave some principal to a beneficiary?

always document the final outcome with a letter to the client that says, in effect, "we met, we talked about these things, here's what I recommended, and here's what you decided to do." Such follow-up letters (also known as discovery agreements) can save an agent many headaches (not to mention errors and omissions problems) down the road.

In fact, an agent probably should document all client meetings with a follow-up letter, and should make notes on any conversations with the client or the carrier with regards to the client.

Sometimes, in order to find the best policy for the customer, an agent must go outside of his or her primary company or companies. In this case, agents might want to work with a brokerage that has a good mix of companies (stock and mutual), a good reputation for service, and proactive marketing and underwriting. A good agency will have underwriting departments qualified to discuss difficult medical situations and who can provide advice on whether or not a difficult case can be underwritten.

Suitability

Suitability means that the purchase recommendations made by the insurance agent are based on reasonable grounds that are "suitable" for the customer. The National Association of Securities Dealers (NASD) defines suitability as "purchase recommendations that are based on information furnished by the customer about the customer's financial situation, needs, and investment objectives." Similarly, the Securities and Exchange Commission defines suitable recommendations as "those made on the basis of the client's needs, financial circumstances, and investment objectives."

Determining the suitability of a particular insurance product for a particular client is arguably the most important service the agent provides. Yet it is also a gray area — controversial, difficult to evaluate, and above all, difficult to regulate.

Two states so far (North Dakota and Minnesota) have begun applying suitability considerations to life insurance sales. Vague references to "suitability" have also sprung up in other state laws having to do with sales of insurance products to senior consumers, such as Medicare supplement and long-term care insurance. The regulations generally specify that the agent selling the insurance must have "reasonable grounds" for believing the recommendation is "suitable" for the customer, based upon the customer's circumstances, risk tolerance, need for insurance, and existing insurance already owned. In California, agents soliciting seniors for long term care and Medicare supplement insurance must make "reasonable efforts to determine whether the purchase is appropriate for the client."

A January 1995 article in *Money* magazine exploring fraudulent sales practices in the sale of life insurance recommended that insurers adopt the principle of suitability, making it illegal for agents to sell products that are inappropriate for a client's financial needs. Such suitability requirements would impose a degree of care (and liability) on agents that has until now merely been implied.

Fiduciary Responsibilities

An agent has a fiduciary responsibility to just about any person or organization with whom he or she comes into contact as part of the day-to-day business of transacting insurance: the insured, the insurer, the applicant for insurance, current clients, etc.

State laws and agency contracts prescribe the agent's specific fiduciary duties. Most agents maintain a separate "premium account" into which they deposit premium payments and from which they remit premiums to the principal and pay return premiums to insureds.

It is unlawful to mingle funds in the premium account with personal funds or funds held in any other capacity. It is likewise unlawful to treat the premium account as personal or business assets, to use it as collateral for a loan, or consider it as either income or assets on the agent's financial statements.

There is usually a specific time period within which premiums must be forwarded to the insurer (for example, in Colorado this is 45 days if there is no contractual due date). Accurate records must be kept of all fiduciary transactions.

As a fiduciary, the agent has an obligation to act in the best interest of the insured. The agent must be knowledgeable about the features and provisions of various insurance policies as well as knowing the use of these insurance contracts. The agent must be able to explain the important features of these policies to the insured. The agent must

Fiduciary Defined

A **fiduciary** is a person in a position of financial trust. Thus, attorneys, CPAs, bank trust officers, and insurance agents are all considered fiduciaries.

Fee-Related Violations

In a December 1995 disciplinary action by the New York Insurance Department, a New York resident agent who collected service fees from insureds without first obtaining their written authorization had his license revoked (he also had failed to forward premiums to the insurance company). Another New York agent/broker who charged service fees without prior authorization was fined $500.

recognize the importance of dealing with the general public's financial needs and problems and offering solutions to these problems through the purchase of insurance products.

The agent must know and comply with the state's insurance laws. Many of these laws are for consumer protection. It is the agent's duty to comply with these laws and thus protect the interests of the insured at all times.

Fiduciary Foul-Ups

If there was a contest to see what violation agents commit most frequently, fiduciary foul-ups would win hands down. A few examples from the state enforcement files:

- ✔ Improperly withheld, misappropriated, or converted to his own use money belonging to a policyholder (Nebraska - $500 administrative fine)
- ✔ Collected premiums and failed to forward them to the appropriate insurer (New York - license revoked)
- ✔ Issued premium checks that were dishonored by the bank, commingled premiums (New York - $1,250 fine)
- ✔ Maintained a negative balance in premium account (New York - license revoked)
- ✔ Conversion of insured's funds (New York - license revoked)
- ✔ Wrongfully availed himself of the proceeds of refund checks (New York - license revoked)

Charging Fees

It is generally illegal for an agent or broker to charge fees in addition to the policy premium for services which are not "truly" extra. There are regulatory constraints against charging additional fees on top of regular policy premium. In many states, it is illegal for any person or insurer to collect premiums or make charges which are "not specified in the insurance contract".

Additional charges may not be made for services which a producer would normally be expected to perform in connection with the sale of an insurance policy (such as evaluating the applicant's needs, recommending coverages, and processing the application).

Extra services for which additional charges may be permitted are those which are not in the scope of the producer's regular duties. These may include special research activities, or services performed as a convenience to the insured where the producer incurs extra additional expenses which are to be passed on to the insured. Usually, if an agent or broker is going to perform and charge for an extra service, the service and the amount to be charged must be specified in a written agreement, and it must be approved by the applicant or insured prior to performance of the service.

While insurance agents traditionally have been paid based on a company's commission structure, this appears to be changing due to case law, advisory opinions, and industry practice. A transition from commission-based compensation to fee-based compensation, as subject to contractual and regulatory (state-by-state) constraints may be occurring, at least in some areas of the industry.

The increased sophistication of insurance consumers demands more information and service from the agent. This, combined with reduced commission levels from insurance companies, is leading agents to consider charging fees for service.

The transition is complicated by ethical issues. Agents are counseled to apply commonsense guidelines to determine whether fee-based compensation is appropriate. Among the determining factors: the annual premium, client expectations, increased resources necessary, and whether the cost of servicing the client will exceed the prevailing commission. It has been suggested that fee-based compensation should not be considered unless and until the annual premium reaches between $100,000 and $500,000. (This would obviously be applicable to larger commercial lines property and liability insurance.)

Some agency contracts limit or prohibit entirely the charging of unauthorized fees. Doing so can get both the agent and the insurance company in trouble. For one, fees can be includible in the insurance company's premium tax liability, so the insurance company must be notified and give written consent. It is considered safest if brokers/agents either charge a fee or accept a commission payment, but not both. Any "discounting" of established fees could be viewed as a violation of rebating restrictions.

In 1995, an Arizona agent was found to have illegally charged more than 2,500 people a $15 "application" fee when they applied for insurance. Another 841 people were charged for auto club memberships that were misidentified as part of their policies. The agent surrendered his license and paid $134,000 in fines and restitutions. Incidents such as this only increase industry and public resistance to the charging of fees.

Most states allow fees to be charged only after the broker/agent has received written permission in advance from both the insurance company and the client. Other states require producers who want to charge fees to file a request with the insurance department. Some states require a separate license in order for an insurance professional to charge a fee; for example, California prohibits life agents from receiving fees unless they are licensed as and acting in the capacity of a life insurance analyst.

Broker fees are permitted in California, but unethical and abusive practices have prompted one agent association (the American Agents Alliance) to change its code of ethics to provide for full disclosure and limits on the amount that can

Fiduciary Foul-Ups (cont.)

- ✔ Failed to deposit premiums in a designated premium account (New York - license revoked)
- ✔ Misappropriating monies of insured (Ohio - license revoked)
- ✔ Misappropriation of premium (Pennsylvania - $1,000 penalty, 5 year license supervision)
- ✔ Premium theft (Pennsylvania - revocation, restitution, 5-year future supervision)
- ✔ Failing to forward premium money (Vermont - license revoked)
- ✔ Failing to promptly forward refunds to applicants (Wisconsin - $2,000 fine and 21-day license suspension)
- ✔ Utilizing premiums for his or her own use (Wisconsin - $500 fine and restitution, revocation of license)
- ✔ Failing to submit applications and premiums to the insured promptly (Wisconsin - $750 and 21-day license suspension)

be charged. "I have heard cases of brokers charging an $800 brokers fee on a $1,300 premium for a personal auto policy," said Lorelle Hurlbut, executive director. "...Is that reflective of the work required of the broker in writing such a risk? I don't think so, and I'm fairly certain the department (of insurance) doesn't either."

Taking the Policy Application

In many insurance sales, the agent accepts the application for the insurance policy from the applicant, and serves as the primary collector of underwriting information for the carrier. What is important for an agent to remember during the application, underwriting, and policy issue process for any insurance policy is that there are equal obligations toward the applicant and the home office insurer. In addition, the agent is responsible for providing the insurance applicant with privacy notices and information such as the Notice of Insurance Information Practices, and finally to provide the insurance applicant with necessary receipts for the initial premium collected.

Confidentiality of Client Information

When taking an application for insurance coverage, the agent becomes privy to certain personal, financial, and even medical information about the applicant. The insurance agent owes the applicant an obligation of confidentiality with regard to any information collected on the application or with regards to claims processing.

That means restricting access to client records to those employees with a legitimate business reason, and documenting office procedures for confidentiality and privacy protection. It is critical that financial and other information on clients is not divulged to anyone, including outside lawyers and accountants, in the absense of due legal process or the written consent of the client.

Insurers are increasingly using very sophisticated, but more non-traditional sources of information for consumer risk assessment, such as consumer credit files, motor vehicle reports, claims histories, etc. At times it is the insurance agent who collects the information at the point of sale, (especially when evaluating new personal lines insurance applications) so it is important for these agents to be aware of the requirements of the Fair Credit Reporting Act, the rights of consumers, and how to resolve consumer disputes. (These responsibilities, which still fall primarily to the insurance company, are covered in detail in Chapter 4.) As an agent, what you are most likely to be called upon to answer are questions like:

- ✔ "Why was my application for insurance turned down?"
- ✔ "Why is the premium I was quoted lower than the premium on the issued policy?

Collecting the Initial Premium

Life and health insurance agents are generally encouraged to collect the initial premium with the application. Evidence shows that this procedure is most effective in having the insured accept the policy when it is issued. If the insured does not pay the initial premium at the time of application, chances increase that he or she will not accept the issued policy.

An important point that the agent should make to the applicant is that if the applicant waits to pay the premium, he or she may become uninsurable, or may die before the policy takes effect. When the initial premium is not paid with the application, no contract is in force. The applicant is not making an offer to the insurer. He or she is merely inviting the insurer to make an offer by issuing the policy.

Since there is no insurance in force under these circumstances, when the agent delivers the policy and collects the initial premium, there may be additional underwriting requirements which must be satisfied. Most commonly, the insurance company may require that the insured sign a health statement verifying that no change in health has occurred since the date of the application.

A 1994 court case demonstrated the importance of this issue. In 1991, Joseph Ryan, Sr., was 63 years old and suffering from emphysema. Expecting his medical costs to be high, he and his children applied for a $100,000 term insurance policy. Everyone present, including the agent, knew of Ryan's poor health. The agent completed the application, collected the first month's premium of $107, and issued a receipt, but neglected to inform the family that a medical examination would be required. The family claimed the agent told them "If your father died right now, you would get $100,000." (The agent later claimed he couldn't remember whether he'd said this.)

The receipt given to the family clearly stated "... If a medical examination is required, no coverage [except for accidental death] will be provided until the examination has been completed." and "(Insurance Company) will grant Temporary Insurance to each person to be insured if at least one month's premium is received on the date of the application and there is no material misrepresentation in the application.... But, if a medical examination of a person to be in-

Advice to Agents: Never Make or Accept Loans from Clients

An insurance agent is persuaded to lend money to a customer, or persuades a customer to loan the agent money, or, in a more subtle twist, persuades a customer to designate the agent as the policy beneficiary.

Who engages in such poor business practices? You'd be surprised. Mixing personal finance and business is bad business, especially when you are a fiduciary.

What can go wrong? An agent in New York was owed money by an insured. When the insured failed to pay him back, the agent surrendered the insured's life insurance policy without permission and kept the cash value as payment for the loan (the policy had been used as collateral for the loan). The agent was fined $1,000.

A Wisconsin agent who borrowed in excess of $20,000 from a client failed to pay it back and had his license revoked.

Equifax

Equifax, a consumer reporting agency used extensively in insurance underwriting, offers automated risk assessment and selection whereby information on the application is evaluated alongside Equifax's own data on the applicant, analyzed according to the insurance carrier's pre-defined underwriting criteria, and an immediate recommendation is made to accept, rate, or decline.

Agents are able to use personal computers to access these automated risk assessment, scoring, and rating processes. Equifax has developed a training course for insurance agents, outlining proper use of these systems and covering the consumer protection requirements imposed by state law and the Fair Credit Reporting Act. (Equifax, 1-800-456-6004)

sured is initially required by our underwriting rules, coverage on that person will not start until completion of the examination."

The agent later informed Ryan's daughter that a medical examination was required on her father before the insurance carrier would issue the policy. She made an appointment for her father to undergo a physical, but Ryan died of a heart attack before the physical was completed. The insurer denied Ryan's application on the grounds that the medical examination was not completed, but the family claimed it was due benefits under the policy. The insurer rejected the claim and returned the first month's premium. The family sued, claiming coverage based on the agent's statements at the time of application. The court supported the company's denial of the claim.

Policy Delivery

The agent is responsible for delivering the insurance policy to the insured and (many times) also collects any premium which may be due at the time of policy delivery. Because some coverages do not take effect until the policy is delivered, timely delivery is critical.

It is considered a good business practice to arrange for personal delivery of the policy. The agent should take the time to explain all policy provisions, particularly the exclusions, and any riders that may restrict the coverage given in the policy, review the purpose of the policy and how it fits into the policyowner's total insurance plan, reinforce the relationship and good will established with the client, explain the possible need for additional coverage, explain how the agency provides ongoing service (such as annual reviews), and even ask the insured for referrals.

Most states require the insurer to provide for a "free look" period (usually 10 days) during which a life insurance policyholder may review the policy and make a final decision regarding the policy (and may receive a full refund if they decide not to keep it). The free look period begins on the date of policy delivery, so it is important to fully explain the details of the free-look provision, and to acknowledge any request for a refund promptly.

Policy delivery is the ideal time to cross check the newly issued policy against what coverage the applicant requested.

Agents should pay particular attention to any riders, endorsements and optional coverages. If the policy has been issued with any changes or amendments, the agent will also be required to explain these changes and obtain the insured's signature acknowledging receipt of these amendments.

With life and health insurance policies, if a conditional receipt has not been previously issued, the insurer may require the agent to obtain a statement of good health at the time of policy delivery.

Legally, the policy is considered "delivered" when it is mailed or turned over to the policyowner or someone acting on his or her behalf. Some companies do mail policies directly to policyowners. However, many prefer to have the agent make a personal delivery.

In some cases, a **constructive delivery** is deemed to occur when the insurer mails a policy to its agent for actual delivery to the policyowner, because the insurer has issued the policy and released it for delivery. However, a legal delivery has not yet occurred if the insurer requires personal delivery for verification of good health at the time of delivery, or if the policy is being provided to the applicant merely to review and inspect at that time, and not necessarily to buy.

Once the policy is delivered, the agent should wrap up any concluding paperwork and complete the policyholder's files.

Advice to Agents: Always Collect the Initial Premium

"One of the worst situations I was ever in didn't even involve a death claim," says Morton Feld, CLU, a California agent and insurance teacher. "I took a life insurance application up in rodeo country from a team roper who had been bedridden for about six months after a fall from his horse. He had improved significantly, was walking again, and the prognosis was good. But he was in the process of closing one bank account and opening another, so I couldn't collect the initial premium with the application.

"When I delivered the policy a few three weeks later, his sister answered the door and explained he had taken a turn for the worse, was bedridden again, and the prognosis was now not very good.

"I could have just left the policy with her, or just mailed the policy and said I wasn't aware of the relapse. Could I have gotten away with relying on constructive delivery? Sure. But I sent the policy back to the company. Then I called the applicant and explained why I couldn't deliver the policy. Amazingly, he understood."

Claims Handling

Agents and agency employees are usually the first to be notified when a client experiences a loss and wants to know whether and how the loss will be paid. Claims are easier to settle when agents provide guidance to the policyholder throughout the claims process. Consumers are less apt to file complaints when they feel their claims are being handled properly. An agent's responsibilities at claims time are relatively straightforward — but still very important.

Certain types of losses, such as a fire, might leave a client without insurance records. In other situations, such as serious injuries to family members due to an automobile accident, a client might have trouble thinking clearly. It is during these times of loss that the accurate records and claim processing knowledge of the agent are most needed. By helping the policyholder submit a timely, detailed, and accurate claim, the agent can minimize settlement delays and misunderstandings. At times it may be necessary to follow up on claims, and to exert a special effort designed to speed relief for loss victims who may be experiencing unusual hardships.

Regardless of the type of insurance, the insurer will usually require a written notice of loss or claim and supporting documents. Most insurance policies contain loss provisions or a section spelling out the **insured's duties when loss occurs**.

Insurers usually provide claim forms on request. Depending upon the type of loss, a variety of special requirements may apply: for a life insurance claim, a death certificate may be required; for an accident or disability claim, a medical examination may be required; for a claim involving theft of insured property, the insurance may not apply if the insured has failed to notify the police of the loss. Property insurance coverages usually require the insured to protect property from further loss. Liability coverages may require that the insurer be notified of claims and suits, even if the lawsuits are groundless. There may be a time limit on when a claim can be filed. The insurer may conduct an investigation before paying a claim.

Various provisions may affect the amount of insurance coverage. For example, in property insurance, a coinsurance clause and the amount of coverage written may determine whether a loss is paid on an actual cash value or replacement cost basis. Many property insurance policies include an **appraisal** clause, which establishes a way to appraise property if the insured and insurer cannot agree on the value or the amount of loss. Automobile insurance policies contain an **arbitration** clause, which establishes a way to settle an uninsured motorists claim if the insured and insurer cannot agree on the amount of loss or whether a person is entitled to payment.

Agents should go over the insured's claim obligations as specified by the insurance policy, such as the obligation to protect property from further damage, the requirement to cooperate with the insurance company, and any requirement to submit a written proof of loss or written claim reports. The client should be told what to expect next from the insurance carrier; when they will be contacted by a claims adjuster, etc.

Notice of loss provided to the insurance agent is considered notice to the carrier, so the agent should transmit notice to the carrier as quickly as possible. If the agent receives notice of a claim but fails to forward it to the company for several weeks, a delay in claims payment could result. Since many state laws require that claims be acknowledged and the appropriate forms be provided to the claimant within 15 days of notice, if agents fail to forward timely notice of claim, the insurance company could be facing market conduct penalties and increased consumer complaints.

Agents should be careful of assuring the policyholder that the loss will be covered unless they are absolutely sure the circumstances of the loss are within the policy's scope of coverage. Agents should not provide legal advice, or make unauthorized decisions on behalf of the insurance company. Agents should also keep track of open claims to help policyholders avoid being affected by any built-in statute of limitations on recovery.

Sometimes, the policyholder disagrees with the insurer's decision to either deny or reduce a claim, which puts the agent in a tough position. The best route is for the agent to share what he or she knows about claims laws, and tell the policyholder how to submit claims disputes to the company, and if necessary, to the state insurance department.

Unfair Trade Practices

The Unfair Trade Practices Act, first introduced by the NAIC in 1947, has been continuously updated and variously adopted by the states. The Act is generally divided into two parts — Unfair Marketing Practices and Unfair Claims Practices. In each state, statutes define and prohibit certain trade and claims practices which are unfair, misleading and deceptive, including sales and marketing practices, discrimination in rating and underwriting, policy cancellation and nonrenewal, and claims investigation and settlement. While most of these laws are directed mostly towards insurance carriers, there are requirements specifically applying to insurance agents.

Below is a brief summary of the prohibited unfair practices that relate to agent behavior that most states have adopted. For more detailed information about what is required by a particular state, refer to that state's unfair practices laws and regulations. This list is by no means exhaustive. Keep in mind that any act can be considered an unfair practice upon investigation by the insurance department, regardless of whether the practice is specifically defined or prohibited by law. If the commissioner believes an agent or insurer is engaging in an unfair method of competition, act, or practice, a hearing may be called to investigate further.

Misrepresentations

A misrepresentation, simply defined, is a lie. It is a violation for any person to make, issue, or circulate any illustration, sales material, or to make any statement which is false, misleading or deceptive. Misrepresentations include (but are not limited to):

- ✔ Misrepresenting the benefits, advantages or terms of any policy
- ✔ Misrepresenting policy dividends or shares of surplus by implying or stating that they are guaranteed

- ✔ Misrepresenting the financial condition of an insurer by means of an inaccurate or incomplete financial comparison
- ✔ Misrepresenting an insurance policy by using any name or title which is untrue or misleading or by indicating that an insurance policy represents shares of stock

Agents have been found guilty of misrepresentation for things like assuring clients that they have coverage when in fact they do not.

False or Deceptive Advertising

It is unlawful for any person to formulate or use an advertisement or make a statement which is untrue, deceptive or misleading regarding any insurer or person associated with an insurer.

"We have seen advertising which compares interest rates between certificates of deposit and life insurance cash values," says one regulator, "which is apples and oranges as far as we're concerned." A Texas regulator reports having seen sales campaigns that advise agents NOT to identify themselves as insurance agents.

The crackdown on market conduct has had a profound effect on how sales materials are developed and used. The days when agents were given freedom and flexibility in creating individualized presentations are over. Now, the home office wants greater control. Many companies allow only the use of preapproved sales materials, and may provide agents with sample preapproved letters and brochures on agent letterhead. Approved documents receive control numbers with expiration dates. Some companies receive and review upwards of 1,000 pieces of sales material each month to be sure they are in compliance.

The Pennsylvania Insurance Department, in its compliance review of Prudential's regional home offices, found that the majority of the unlawful advertising materials were prepared by agents, not by the insurer. Prudential had a company policy which required agents to receive company approval before distributing such ads; but the policy was never enforced.

Agents should not assume that documents provided by the company in the past are still approved for use; agents should verify the approval status of any document about which they are not completely sure.

Twisting/Churning

Twisting is illegally inducing a person to drop existing insurance in order to purchase similar coverage with another agent or company (also called external replacement). For example, an agent may misrepresent another insurer by falsely making statements about the financial condition of the company or by giving an incomplete comparison of policies. This misrepresentation (illegal inducement) is used to persuade a person to drop existing coverage and purchase insurance with a different agent.

Churning is another word for improper policy replacement, but it involves replacing policies within the same company (internal replacement). The typical churning "victim" would be someone who has a significant amount of cash value and/or accumulated dividends in an existing policy. Florida began investigating the practice of churning in 1995 after Tampa residents complained they had been sold new policies without being informed that the new policy premiums would be paid out of the cash values of a policy being replaced. In some cases, the consumers lost all of the savings in the older policy.

Congressional hearings have been held to examine the practice of churning in the life insurance industry. Companies and agents have been accused of using fraudulent sales pitches that conceal vital information, or promise unrealistically optimistic future returns on policy values (so-called "vanishing" premiums).

False Financial Statements

It is a violation for any person to deliberately make a false financial statement regarding the solvency of an insurer with the intent to deceive others. An agent could be found in violation for telling an applicant that the insurance company with whom the coverage is being placed is financially stable when in fact its financial condition has been downgraded or declining steadily.

Rebating

Rebating is also considered a violation of the Unfair Trade Practices Act in most states (Florida and California being notable exceptions). Rebating is defined as any inducement in the sale of insurance which is not specified in the insurance contract. The offer of sharing commissions with the insurance applicant is an inducement in the sale of insurance which is not part of the insurance policy and thus, rebating. Rebates include not only cash but also personal services and items of value.

This means that during any insurance transaction, and even when advertising, agents must not offer a free gift, bonus, or anything of value outside of the policy or contract, which is

Free Dental Not Part of the Contract

A Pennsylvania life and health insurance company developed a new marketing campaign. Individuals purchasing a health insurance policy would be provided with free dental insurance.

Unfortunately, the free dental insurance constituted an inducement to buy which was "not part of the regular contract".

The result: The company entered into a consent order to cease and desist and paid a $5,000 penalty to the state.

Penalties for Defamation and False Financial Statements

In Pennsylvania, an agent who misrepresented the financial condition of an insurance company and made false statements was fined $10,000 and given five years of license supervision.

an inducement to buy. State laws differ on how "anything of value" is defined.

California's anti-rebate provisions were repealed when the controversial Proposition 103 was passed. Florida permits rebating in certain situations, under a rebate schedule which must be filed by the agent and which must be applied "uniformly" to those purchasing a policy from the agent.

While some agents believe they should be able to voluntarily relinquish part of their commission if it will help them close a sale, others believe that allowing rebates encourages unethical behavior and gives an unfair advantage to larger agencies that can better afford to give up income.

Defamation

It is unlawful for any person or company to be maliciously critical or derogatory about any insurer or person associated with an insurer. This includes oral statements and written statements contained in any literature which are circulated for the purpose of doing personal injury to any person or company's good name and reputation.

Agents should find out what the company's policy is regarding product comparisons to competitors' products. If they are permitted, then the agent should be sure to make fair comparisons, and avoid comparing policies that do not share common features.

Discrimination

It is unlawful to permit discrimination between individuals of the same class or insurance risk in terms of rates, premiums, fees and policy benefits, based on their place of residence, race, creed or national origin.

For underwriting purposes, discrimination is prohibited when based on race, religion, nationality, ethnic group, age, sex, family size, occupation, place of residence, or marital status. However, underwriting standards may be based on actuarially sound principles (such as statistical proof that women live longer than men, or that younger drivers are higher risk than older drivers, thus affecting the level of risk).

This means that neither the insurer nor the agent may cancel, limit, or refuse to insure or renew insurance coverage based on unfairly discriminatory standards. Primary responsibility for compliance with this law falls with the insurance carrier. Agents and brokers should be familiar with the anti-discrimination laws and should refuse to comply with insurers engaged in discriminatory sales or underwriting.

Boycott, Coercion or Intimidation

It is a violation for any person or organization to commit or be involved in any act of boycott, coercion or intimidation which is intended to create a monopoly or restrict fair trade in the transaction of insurance.

For example, it is unlawful for a lending institution to force a person to purchase insurance from a particular company or agent as a condition for receiving a loan. (Likewise, an agent cannot participate in such illegal coercion by being the agent from whom coverage must be purchased as a precondition to obtaining the loan.) The lending institution may require that adequate insurance be purchased or be in force to back such a loan but the lending institution cannot force or intimidate a person into purchasing coverage from a specific insurer as a condition for the granting of a loan.

Lowballing: Unfair Trade Practice in New York

New York agents are often penalized for "lowballing", an unfair trade practice involving premium misquotes.

The New York Auto Insurance Plan Rating Manual is used for determining automobile insurance premiums. Lowballing occurs when an agent intentionally misquotes premium information to the consumer and accepts a low deposit just to get the business (and undercut the competition). The consumer is eventually billed by the insurance carrier for the difference.

New York's Department of Insurance actively pursues complaints against agents for lowballing. The result is often license revocation.

COMMON UNFAIR TRADE PRACTICES

✔ **Boycott**. The act of refusing to transact insurance business dealings with another until he or she complies with certain conditions or concessions.

✔ **Defamation**. A false, maliciously critical or derogatory statement intended to injure a person engaged in the insurance business.

✔ **Discrimination**. Allowing differences in rates, premiums, fees and/or policy benefits between individuals of the same class or insurance risk based on place of residence, race, creed or national origin.

✔ **False or Deceptive Advertising**. The formulation or use of an advertisement or statement which is untrue, deceptive or misleading regarding any insurer or person associated with an insurer.

✔ **False Financial Statements**. The deliberate use or creation of false financial documents regarding the solvency of an insurer designed with the intent to deceive others.

✔ **Illegal Premiums or Charges**. Any premium or charge not specified in the insurance contract.

✔ **Misrepresentation**. The use of oral or written statements that do not truly reflect the facts either by an insured on an application for insurance or by an insurer concerning the terms or benefits of an insurance policy.

✔ **Rebating**. Illegal in most states. The returning of a portion of the agent's commission to an insured or anything else of value given an insured as an inducement to buy. The payment of policy dividends, retroactive rate adjustments, and reduced premiums that reflect the savings of direct payment to an agent or home office are not usually considered to be rebates.

✔ **Twisting**. Misrepresenting a policy or making incomplete comparisons of policies to induce a policyowner to change or replace an existing policy.

CHART 2-1

Special Requirements for Life and Health Insurance Sales

In many jurisdictions, special requirements apply to the marketing and advertising of life and health insurance. Minimum standards for advertising life and accident/health insurance assure truthful and adequate disclosure of relevant information, prevent unfair competition among insurers, and encourage accurate presentations and descriptions for the insurance-buying public. Insurers are held responsible for advertisements regardless of who distributes them, which is why corporate compliance offices have become so strict with agent sales materials. Agents should be sure they are using only approved sales materials.

Most states require life and health insurance agents to provide prospective insureds with a **policy summary** and a **buyers guide** at the time of application. A policy summary is a document that summarizes the coverages, benefits, limitations, exclusions, and terms of the policy proposed for sale. A buyers guide is a consumer publication that describes the type of coverage being offered, and provides general information to help the applicant compare different policies and reach a decision about whether the proposed coverage is appropriate. Failure to leave a buyer's guide at the time of policy application as required by state law can result in disciplinary action.

Special Requirements for Sales to Seniors

Because of the complexity of insurance products sold to senior consumers of insurance, and because seniors are seen as a particularly vulnerable segment of the consumer population, there are special regulatory prohibitions applicable to advertising and marketing the types of insurance products sold to seniors. Penalties in addition to any other penalties provided for by law may be imposed for violations committed against seniors. Florida, Illinois, Louisiana, North Carolina, Texas, and Washington are some of the states that make the financial exploitation of an older person a criminal offense.

Among the practices specifically prohibited are **high pressure tactics** and **cold lead advertising**. High pressure tactics refer to any method of marketing which induces the purchase of insurance through force, fright, threat, or other undue pressure. Cold lead advertising makes use of marketing methods which fail to conspicuously disclose that the purpose of the marketing is the solicitation of insurance and that contact will be made by an insurance agent or company.

Those soliciting insurance to seniors may not use true or fictitious names that are deceptive or misleading; and may not imply connection to a government agency, nonprofit or charitable institution, or senior organization to indicate the policy is endorsed by government agencies. Advertisements must not imply that the policyholders will become members of a special class or group and enjoy group privileges, unless such is the case.

Many states prohibit the sale of excessive insurance to seniors, such as duplicate Medicare supplement or long-term care policies, and even limit the commissions paid on first and second year policies, as well as replacement policies. Insurers may be required to report the number of duplicative senior coverages on an annual basis to the insurance department. Also, market conduct examiners may review a company's policyholder records to detect multiple issuance of senior policies.

In 1992 a California agent had his license revoked for selling 19 duplicative and unnecessary policies over a two-year period to an elderly woman. She purchased seven long-term care policies, seven life insurance policies, four Medicare supplement policies, and a cancer policy (the California standard for overloading is any more than two policies). The woman paid out $40,000 in premiums, of which $20,000 went for agent commissions. Then-Commissioner John Garamendi called this "the worst case of abuse of an insurance consumer imaginable."

In Virginia, an agent was found intimidating older people to buy two, three, or four of the same kinds of policies from different insurance companies. The agent falsified the part of the application that asks whether the person already has similar insurance coverage. In response to a complaint, the DOI found substantial evidence of wrongdoing: the agent had backdated policies, told applicants there were complications in the insurer's underwriting procedures that were delaying response, and wrongfully applied premiums from one person's application to another person's policy. The agent was ultimately prosecuted in six jurisdictions for larceny, and received an 18 year prison sentence.

Another Virginia case involved a husband and wife agent team who routinely "loaded up" seniors with policies they didn't need. The DOI received a complaint from a policyholder who purchased two Medicare supplement policies and was told she would be paid twice upon submitting a claim. Upon investigation, the insurance department discovered numerous violations: the couple had sold over 40 duplicative policies to two elderly sisters; even whole life policies where the premiums paid far exceeded the face amount of the policy. The agents surrendered their licenses in lieu of disciplinary action, but the wife was subsequently prosecuted by the U.S. attorney for continued activities involving insurance.

When Is a Sales Practice Deceptive?

Industry representatives all agree that consumers have a right to expect responsible sales tactics when they consider purchasing insurance. But not all deceptive sales practices are as obvious as those outlined above. "What is crafty marketing to an insurance company or agent may be false and misleading conduct to an insurance regulator," warns Art Chartrand, former counsel for market conduct at the NAIC. An important question for an agent to ask is "What would I consider a deceptive sales practice?" And more importantly, "Among the sales practices I use, could any be construed to be unfair?"

Considering how unfamiliar consumers are with the principles underlying insurance contracts, even a technically accurate product description may be too confusing for the average buyer. If the customer misunderstands the provisions, coverages, exclusions, and limitations of his or her policy, the sales practice used may be considered misleading.

For example, a proposal presented to a customer that is titled "Retirement Funding Proposal" or "Private Pension Plan" might be ruled misleading even the "plan" proposed is a life insurance policy, even if the policy has a 30-day free look, and even if the cover sheet instructs the individual to read the entire policy carefully.

Researchers for LIMRA (Life Insurance Marketing & Research Association) International have concluded that no single piece of sales literature or statement made by the agent needs to be incorrect in order for the sales process to be considered deceptive. If the net result of a sales practice is a pattern of customer misunderstanding, then the entire sales process can be viewed as deceptive. (Most experts acknowledge that the occasional individual consumer will misinterpret product features; deceptive practices become more evident when multiple policyholders experience similar misunderstandings.)

Unfair Claims Practices

While Unfair Claims Practices are considered part of the Unfair Trade Practices Act, and are important for agents to understand, we will discuss them in detail in a later chapter, as part of the insurance company's responsibilities towards policyholders. However, this act can also be applied to any agent who adjusts losses.

When an agent is notified of a claim by a policyholder, it is his or her obligation as the legal representative of the insurance company, to expedite necessary communications between the insurance company claims department and the policyholder. Following an investigation and a hearing, if the insurance department finds that any person or insurer is engaged in any unfair trade or unfair claims practice, a cease and desist order may be issued which prohibits the individual or company from continuing the practice. Failure to comply with a cease and desist order can result in a substantial fine (usually $10,000, but these amounts differ by state). In addition, fines and loss of license may also be imposed for any company or person guilty of violating the act.

Replacement Questionnaire

The American Society of CLU & ChFC has developed a six-page Replacement Questionnaire (RQ), designed to help agents determine when replacement is in the client's best interest. The questionnaire provides agents with a consistent, impartial method for evaluating the key issues (regulatory, legal, and taxation) relative to policy replacement. By creating a responsible approach for fact collection, professional analysis, and recommendations for informed decision-making, the Society hopes the questionnaire will help agents and clients alike better manage the replacement dilemma. (Contact: American Society of CLU & ChFC, 270 Bryn Mawr Avenue, Bryn Mawr PA 19010, 800-392-6900).

Replacement

Replacement, simply, is the purchase of one insurance policy to replace another. Because of the cash values that can build up in a life insurance policy, and the favorable loan interest rates in older policies, replacement can be disadvantageous to consumers. However, there are good reasons to replace a policy, particularly if it does not meet the current needs of the consumer.

Insurance industry experts differ widely in their opinions on replacement. Some say replacements are almost universally bad for consumers. Others argue that it's much worse to keep obsolete policies in force.

Commissions paid to agents for selling a new life insurance policy are particularly lucrative. For this reason, unscrupulous agents have persuaded consumers to give up old policies for new ones, even if it was not in the best interests of the policyholder.

Life insurance policy replacement can be costly to the policyholder, not only because a new commission must be paid on the new sale, but also because policies are intended to stay in force for many years in order to build up cash values. But it is quite possible that replacement can benefit the policyholder, because of new product features, improvements, new preferred rating eligibility, or even because the current insurer is experiencing financial woes and the policyholder would be safer with another carrier. Agents sometimes see policies they sold replaced because they have been remiss in providing continuing service and advice to the client, and the client moves their business to a more responsive agent.

Carriers may oppose the replacement of older policies because older policies are more profitable; the acquisition costs and sales and marketing costs have already been absorbed. They also don't want agents who move to another carrier to take all their business with them. Some carrier-agent contracts include anti-replacement clauses intended to restrict improper replacement, but it's up to the company to determine what is improper. Some contracts reduce commissions for internally replaced business; others prohibit the agent from inducing a current policyholder from replacing coverage.

How big a problem is replacement? ACLI reports the number

of ordinary life policies that traditionally lapse within the first two years is about 20%. A.M. Best reports the industry's overall lapse ratio at between 9-10%. A study by the Life Insurance and Marketing Research Association (LIMRA) indicates that 14% of all life insurance new sales involved replacement of an existing policy. Researchers added that the percentage is probably higher (30% by some estimates) because of difficulty in tracking all replaced business. (Other studies have shown that agents may be unaware they are replacing a policy when writing new business!)

Recognizing that replacement will remain a front burner issue, the NALU has formed a task force on replacement which will attempt to distinguish between wise and ethical replacement of life insurance policies and unwarranted "twisting" of policies. The task force intends to develop guidelines for reform and enforcement. One recommendation being considered is "renewal-only" level commissions for replaced policies. NALU has also suggested strengthening disclosure and notification requirements, such as extending the "free look" period to 60 days for replacement policies. In New York, proposed legislation designed to strengthen consumer protections during replacement may delay the payment of commissions on life insurance policies until after the 60-day "cooling off" period.

Replacement Regulation

When replacement of life insurance is involved, the agent must comply with all pertinent federal and state regulations. Each state has rules and regulations regarding replacement of life insurance products which are designed to protect the interests of the insuring public. Frequently, it is not in the best interests of the insured to replace existing life insurance with a new policy. The reasons for this are many:

- ✔ New insurance requires the applicant to prove insurability
- ✔ Premiums may be higher for a new policy
- ✔ New policy provisions will have to be complied with such as a new incontestable period
- ✔ The existing policy's provisions may be more liberal than a new policy's provisions
- ✔ Generally, a new policy will not have any current cash values

The National Association of Insurance Commissioners (NAIC) has adopted a Model Life Insurance Replacement Regulation. Upwards of 40 states have adopted replacement regulations based on this model.

Duties of Agents and Brokers

Replacement is defined by the NAIC model act as any transaction in which new life insurance or a new annuity is to be purchased, and it is known, or should reasonably be known to the agent or broker, or to the insurer if there is no agent, that as part of the transaction, existing life insurance or annuity will be:

- ✔ Lapsed, forfeited, surrendered, or terminated
- ✔ Converted to reduced paid-up insurance continued as extended term insurance, or reduced in value by the use of nonforfeiture benefits or other policy values
- ✔ Amended to produce a reduction in the benefits or in the term for which coverage would otherwise remain in force, or for which benefits would be paid
- ✔ Reissued with reduction in cash value

Generally, the duties of the agent or broker include: obtaining, along with the application, a signed statement from the applicant as to whether or not insurance is to be replaced; and submitting the statement to the insurer.

If replacement is involved, the agent or broker is required to:

- ✔ List all existing life insurance policies to be replaced
- ✔ Give the applicant a completed **Comparison Statement**, signed by the agent or broker, and a **Notice to Applicants Regarding Replacement of Life Insurance** (a copy of the forms should be left with the applicant)
- ✔ Give the insurer a copy of any proposals made, and a copy of the Comparison Statement with the name of insurer that is to be replaced

The agent must take special care when replacing an existing policy with a new policy to make sure that the insured is not misled into purchasing a policy which is to the insured's disadvantage. The agent also needs to be aware of his or her own errors and omissions liability, particularly in the area of replacement.

Duties of the Insurer

The duties of the replacing insurer include:

- ✔ Making sure that all replacement actions are in compliance with state regulations
- ✔ Notifying each insurer whose insurance is being replaced and upon request, furnishing a copy of any proposal and Comparison Statement

- ✔ Maintaining copies of proposals, receipts and Comparison Statements

Each individual state has established time limits for the performance of duties. Agents should check state regulations to learn specific time limits, such as:

- ✔ The time within which an agent must supply the applicant with a Comparison Statement
- ✔ The time and manner within which the agent must notify the insurer of replacement activities
- ✔ The time within which the insurer must notify the insurer being replaced that such action is in operation
- ✔ The time within which the insurer being replaced must respond to the replacing insurer and the applicant

Most states also require a "free look" period (averaging 20-30 days) during which the client has the right to a full refund of premiums if he or she decides not to keep the new policy for any reason.

What Can Go Wrong

In September 1983, Peter van der Heyde purchased a $200,000 whole life insurance policy. A year later, with the policy up for renewal, van der Heyde's agent suggested replacing the policy with a $200,000 life policy from a different insurer. Van der Heyde, who was in his mid-fifties, did so and allowed the first policy to lapse. Although the same agent had sold the original policy, he neglected to mention that policy on the application for the new policy, and indicated on the application that the insured did not intend that the new policy "replace or change any existing insurance."

Approximately 22 months after the issuance of the policy, van der Heyde killed himself. The insurer refused to pay policy benefits based on the two-year suicide exclusion. (Benefits would have been payable under the original policy, regardless of suicide, had it remained in effect.) The insured's wife sued for benefits, and the insurance company settled with her after the appeals court determined the agent had failed to comply with replacement regulations, and the agent knew or should have known that the second policy was a replacement policy.

Intracompany Replacement

One would assume there is no benefit to the insured (and great benefit to the agent) when an insurance policy undergoes *intracompany replacement* (is replaced by a similar policy with the same insurer). Therefore, most general agency and agent contracts specify that the agent's commission will be limited to a percentage of the increase in premium only when a policy is replaced within the same company. This discourages the agent from replacing existing policies with new policies from the same insurer unless the amounts of coverage (and thus the premium) are substantially increased.

Life Policy Replacement Requirements for Agents & Insurers

State	Number of Days for Free Look	Number of Days for Free Look in Replacements	Time Period for keeping Replacement Records
Alabama	*	20	3 yrs
Alaska	*	*	*
Arizona	*	20	3 yrs
Arkansas	*	*	3 yrs
California	to be set by insurer between 10 to 30	20	3 yrs
Colorado	15	20	3 yrs
Connecticut	10	*	3 yrs
Delaware	10	20	3 yrs
District of Columbia	*	*	*
Florida	10 if no Buyers Guide before taking premium	10 if no Buyers Guide before taking premium	3 yrs
Georgia	10	10	3 yrs
Hawaii	10	10	3 yrs
Idaho	20	20	3 yrs
Illinois	10	20	3 yrs
Indiana	10	20	3 yrs
Iowa	10 (if applicant over age of 60, then 30 days)	20	3 yrs
Kansas	10	20	3 yrs
Kentucky	10	30	3 yrs
Louisiana	10	20	3 yrs
Maine	10	*	*
Maryland	10	20	3 yrs
Massachusetts	10	20	3 yrs
Michigan	10	10	3 yrs
Minnesota	limitation must be disclosed	*	*
Mississippi	10	20	3 yrs
Missouri	10	20	3 yrs
Montana	10	20	3 yrs
Nebraska	10	20	3 yrs
Nevada	10	10	3 yrs
New Hampshire	10	*	3 yrs
New Jersey	10	20	5 yrs
New Mexico	10	*	*
New York	10	*	3 yrs
North Carolina	10	10	3 yrs
North Dakota	20	*	*
Ohio	10	20	3 yrs
Oklahoma	10	20	3 yrs
Oregon	*	20	3 yrs
Pennsylvania	10	20	3 yrs
Rhode Island	10	20	3 yrs
South Carolina	10	20	3 yrs
South Dakota	10	*	*
Tennessee	10	20	5 yrs
Texas	*	*	*
Utah	10	20	3 yrs
Vermont	10	20	3 yrs
Virginia	10	*	*
Washington	10	20	3 yrs
West Virginia	10	30	3 yrs
Wisconsin	30	20	3 yrs
Wyoming	*	20	3 yrs

* = Not Available.

CHART 2-2

Replacement of Health Insurance

Agents attempting to replace an insured's health insurance policy with a new policy need to take special care not to mislead the insured or provide coverage which is to the insured's detriment. Of particular concern is the fact that health conditions covered under an insured's existing policy may not be covered under a replacement policy because of the exclusion of **preexisting conditions**, or new **waiting periods** may be established.

"No loss-no gain" legislation requires that when health insurance is replaced, ongoing claims under the former policy must continue to be paid under the new policy, thereby overriding any preexisting conditions exclusion. In replacing group health coverage, a transfer of benefits statement assures that benefits provided under the old policy continue under the new policy.

Because the elderly are extremely vulnerable and often victimized insurance prospects, and are most susceptible to being penalized by preexisting conditions limitations, agents should be aware that there are often more restrictive regulations for replacing Medicare supplement and long-term care policies. For example, in Arizona, when taking an application for long term care insurance, agents must list any other health insurance policies they have sold to the applicant in the past five years. Insurers in Arizona must maintain records for each agent's amount of replacement sales as a percentage of the agent's total annual sales. The top 10% of agents with the greatest percentages of lapses and replacements must be reported to the department of insurance.

Advice to Agents: Explain Policy Provisions

The agent must clearly explain policy provisions such as who is insured (and equally important: who is not), what is covered, what is excluded, etc. by each policy sold, to ensure that there are no misunderstandings at claims time.

If the insured declines a particular coverage, or declines endorsements which the agent has recommended, agents should be sure to get the declination in writing from the insured. Failure to do so can result in errors and omissions claims against the agent.

Disclosure

Property/Casualty Insurance

Perhaps the most important market conduct responsibility for property/casualty agents is disclosure. Property/casualty agents create coverage for clients based on the client's exposures. Such agents are advised to write the broadest possible coverage and anticipate future events.

Insurance vs. Investments

In life insurance, there are distinct and definite "no-nos" when it comes to describing life products. Topping the list of things agents should never say are phrases about investing and investment returns.

When is Life Insurance Not Life Insurance?

"In many instances the problem has been that life insurance hasn't been described as life insurance," agrees ACLI managing counsel Al Dawson. "It's not a piece of the moon, it's not a fabulous investment that's going to yield many times the premium paid, unless, of course, the insured dies." Life insurance is life insurance first and must always be described a being primarily an insurance (protection) product.

While there are investment components to the life insurance purchase, life insurance is primarily a protection tool that receives favorable tax treatment because of that function. Even variable insurance products should always receive primary representation as insurance.

Calling life insurance accumulations "investments" has gotten many agents in trouble, and in fact is expressly prohibited by many state laws. Life insurance is a unique product, and it may seem logical to describe it as one way to accumulate money for retirement, to fund charitable giving or a child's college education, or to function as an investment product, but it's not good business practice and can quickly get agents in trouble.

Premiums are Premiums

Similarly, premiums are premiums and not payments, contributions investments, or deposits. Cash values should never be referred to as equity, savings, passbook savings, liquidity accounts, emergency accounts, or earnings. Agents should never imply that tax-deferred means tax-free. The word "guaranteed" should be used with care, since life insurance buyers do not easily understand which elements of the policy are guaranteed and which are not.

An Agent is An Agent

A life insurance agent is not a financial advisor, financial planner, financial consultant, retirement planner, pension specialist, or investment counselor. Agents must be very clear to identify themselves as representing life insurance companies and make it clear that they sell insurance products.

It is best to say "I provide a variety of insurance and financial products to help individuals and businesses with insurance planning." Also agents must be sure to identify the insurer(s) being represented.

Disclosure Letters and Disclosure Forms

In disclosing the benefits of an insurance policy, an agent must describe the risks as well. Agents must present fair product comparisons and should not extoll the virtues of one product and then dwell on the drawbacks of another. It is best to keep explanations clear and understandable.

Agents are strongly encouraged to use disclosure forms (sign-off forms) and disclosure letters (follow-up letters) to protect all parties — agent, consumer, and carrier — from misunderstandings.

A **disclosure form** describes the product being sold and how it applies to the consumer's needs. This form, which is signed by both the agent and the client at the conclusiont of the actual sales presentation, ensures that all relevant disclosures have been made during the sales presentation. This would include:

- ✔ Information about the insurance company
- ✔ A full description of the policy(ies) presented (including exclusions, limitations, and any charges such as surrender charges or cancellation charges)
- ✔ The "free look" period
- ✔ The Policy Summary (or Outline of Coverage)
- ✔ Buyers Guide
- ✔ Any illustrations used (and a statement that illustrations are estimates and not guarantees of future results)
- ✔ A Prospectus (if a variable product was presented)

If the policy is a replacement policy, the sign-off form should attest that all replacement procedures were properly followed and all replacement forms reviewed and completed.

The **disclosure letter** is mailed to the consumer as a follow-up to the sales presentation. It should summarize what was discussed at the presentation, what types of insurance products the agent proposed to the prospective client, and what final decisions were made. It is important to include documentation of the sales process that was used, the risk assessment performed (such as any fact finders or client needs analysis), the reasons for the recommendations that were made, any product comparisons that were made, details about the policies recommended, and discussion of any illustrations used.

Disclosure letters and forms are extremely important: they help establish that the agent has explained all product features as required by state law. They give the client the opportunity to confirm that he or she understands what has been presented and what has been purchased. They also reduce the possibility that the client will later claim that he or she did not understand what was being purchased. Because questions and problems can surface at any time, it is a good idea to maintain copies of disclosure forms indefinitely. The American Society of CLU & ChFC provides sample disclosure forms. (800-392-6900)

Telephone Solicitation

Federal and state laws regulate solicitations conducted by telephone. Agents who make telephone solicitations must identify themselves as insurance agents and identify the insurer they represent.

Insurance Company Financial Standing

Agents are expected to place coverages for their policyholders in financially sound insurance companies. In spite of the fact that agents are not actuarial experts, agents are increasingly also expected to monitor the continuing financial solvency of the companies with whom they have placed business.

There are several organizations that rate the financial strength of insurance carriers, based on an analysis of a company's claims experience, investment performance, management, and other factors. These organizations include A.M. Best Company, Standard & Poor's Insurance Rating Services, Moody's Investors Service, Duff & Phelps Credit Rating Company, and Weiss Ratings. These ratings are one of the most widely used indicators of financial health (or the lack of it) in the insurance industry.

Guaranty Associations

Protection against insurer insolvency is one of the principal concerns of regulators in the insurance industry. Insurance insolvency regulations govern such areas as the organization and ownership of a new company, capital and surplus requirements, reserves, accounting, investments, annual statements, and the rehabilitation and liquidation of impaired insurers. In addition to these areas of regulation, insurance departments in many states have adopted regulations for the establishment of guaranty associations in the event that an insurer does, in spite of regulations and precautions, become insolvent.

State Guaranty Associations are organized to protect claimants, policyholders, annuitants and creditors of financially impaired or insolvent insurers by providing funds for the payment of claims and other related policy benefits. The Associations are composed of the insurers authorized to transact a particular line of insurance business within the state. Member insurers are assessed certain sums of money (most often based on the percentage of premiums each insurer has individually earned in the state) to cover the Association's operating expenses. If an insurer insolvency should occur, each member insurer is assessed additional fees to cover the insolvency.

Most states prohibit insurance agents from referring to the existence of Guaranty Associations during the insurance advertising or sales process, in order to prevent misunderstandings on the consumers' part that their insurance policies are "guaranteed" or "insured" in the same way that bank deposits are insured by the FDIC.

Agents can walk a fine line between accurately disclosing the existence and purpose of a guaranty association without in any way implying that the insurance product being sold is a "safe investment" because of the existence of the guaranty association.

Policy Illustrations

Policy illustrations are used by agents to demonstrate how the cash values and non-guaranteed elements of a proposed life insurance policy may perform over the life of the policy. While consumers may fail to read the policy and its accompanying sales literature, they will pay attention to illustrations, which use charts and graphs to demonstrate how cash values may grow over a period of time. Illustrations are used to provide general information about the policy being sold, but the buyer often does not see the actual contract until it is delivered, some time after the sale has been made.

Consumers are not economists, accountants, or financial experts, and often do not understand that policy illustrations are estimates of what might happen based on the continuation of a given set of assumptions. Too many assume the numbers used in sales illustrations are a promise or guarantee of the policy's future performance. And although sales illustrations are traditionally accompanied by strong cautionary language indicating that numbers shown are estimates only, consumers often fail to read or understand such language.

Serious problems with life policy illustrations have arisen when the projections used are either overly optimistic (relying on higher interest rates or better investment performance than can reasonably be expected) or are based on more favorable — but not guaranteed — underlying assumptions (such as improved mortality, reduced administrative costs, or preferred risk rates). Consumers can be led to believe that their policy will perform like an investment product, or that premiums will "vanish" after a short period (such as 10 years). Many agents have used "current" values (which tend to project high rates of interest) rather than the values guaranteed by the policy (which are much lower) to illustrate possible future performance of a policy.

Policy Illustrations ... 10 Years Ago

The policy illustrations of the '80s relied on unrealistically high interest rates and unsupportable cash value accumulations that would dazzle even the most skeptical prospect. No wonder agents relied on them so heavily to generate sales: they worked!

But howls of protest from the insurance buying public, which was caught unprepared for the falling interest rates of the late 1980s and early 1990s, have caused insurers to rethink how illustrations are used. Consumer groups have called for a full halt to the practice of using policy illustrations as a sales tool. Agents in turn protest that life insurance sales would be impossible without the use of policy illustrations. Industry experts and regulators are divided over the use — and usefulness — of policy illustrations.

A Tough Sell

"Life insurance isn't easy to sell," acknowledges Paul DeAngelo, director of enforcement and consumer protection at the New Jersey Insurance Department. "And people who do it ethically have an even harder time selling it. The emphasis should be on continuous communication with and education of the consumer by the company and agent over the life of the policy, rather than through policy illustrations used at the time of inception," he recommends.

The 1995 New York Life class action settlement was based on charges of misleading sales practices, particularly misleading policy illustrations. Policyholders sued because their policies didn't keep up with the optimistic projections of the 1980s, because of declining interest rates and other financial developments that prevented the policies from performing as originally illustrated. In settling, the company offered to help policyholders pay their unexpected, supposedly "vanishing" premiums.

Former Texas Insurance Commissioner J. Robert Hunter, in testimony submitted to a 1994 Congressional hearing on deceptive life insurance sales practices, noted that "modern technology has pushed this abuse to new levels. It is now possible for agents to sit down at their personal computers and produce their own illustrations without company review. A few agents have even gone so far as to use the lap-top to exclude the guaranteed column of information to mislead customers."

"Persons who purchased the 'vanishing premium' policy had in hand at the time of purchase an illustration that showed how the system worked," argues Martin Wilson, a former regulator who now provides insurance counsel through the Troutman Sanders law firm in Atlanta. "However, over the course of intervening years, they forgot the details of the system and now claim in hindsight to have been convinced to purchase the product solely because the premium would vanish and never have to be 'paid' again. The illustration they were handed at the time of solicitation or purchase clearly shows the belief to be unfounded, but the insured party has only retained a present memory of the 'highlights' of the presentation (some of which were well over a decade prior to the resurfacing of premiums)."

Clearly, while sales illustrations are useful in demonstrating how policy values can fluctuate under different assumptions, they are of limited use when comparing one insurer's non-guaranteed estimates about its product with another insurer's equally non-guaranteed estimates. One alternative to unreliable sales illustrations is to compare companies and policies based on actual past performance (with the caveat that "past performance is no guarantee of future results").

A New NAIC Model for Policy Illustrations

Concerned that companies and agents were using overly aggressive assumptions in creating their illustrations, in

December 1995 the NAIC adopted a model regulation that provides illustration formats, prescribes standards to be followed when using life insurance illustrations, and specifies the disclosures that are required in connection with illustrations. The goal of the regulation is to make illustrations more understandable, and to make sure that illustrations are not misleading to purchasers of insurance. Although this model will take time to be adopted by state legislatures, and may be modified along the way, it serves as fair warning and good advice for agent conduct during life illustrations.

According to the NAIC model, insurance companies must notify the commissioner of insurance whether a particular policy will be marketed with or without illustrations. If there will be illustrations, an illustration must be delivered to the prospect, and both the agent and prospect must sign a statement indicating they have discussed and understand that non-guaranteed elements of the policy are subject to change and actual results could be higher or lower.

The illustration must include the name of the insurer, agent, proposed insured, underwriting or rating classification on which the illustration is based, generic policy name, initial death benefit, and dividend option or application of non-guaranteed elements. The model regulation also imposes requirements on the insurer to develop more realistic scales for projecting the growth in non-guaranteed elements and cash value, and these scales (current and disciplined) must receive annual approval from the insurance department. The agent may not use illustrations that project more favorable results than those provided by the insurer.

Policy illustrations should have three distinct columns: one illustrating "guaranteed values", one illustrating "current values", and one showing "current return minus 1%".

Agents are prohibited from representing the policy as anything other than a life insurance policy (such as calling it an investment product or retirement vehicle, for example). Agents must take particular care to describe the non-guaranteed elements (such as dividends) clearly, and must not in any way imply that the payment of non-guaranteed elements is guaranteed. Incomplete illustrations are prohibited. Agents may not represent that premium payments are not required every year, and may no longer use terminology such as vanishing premium to imply the policy becomes paid up or that the policyholder can use non-guaranteed elements to pay future premiums. Agents may no longer use illustrations

Selling Ethically

"Selling ethically means an agent's customers understand what they are buying," says Bill Free of the Life Underwriter Training Council. "It's possible to sell without using illustrations, but you **can** use illustrations and sell ethically."

Penalties

In addition to suspension, revocation and nonrenewal of license, an agent may be fined or imprisoned for violation of state insurance laws. Depending on the violation, fines can range from $100 to several thousand dollars. If an agent is in violation of civil law, the insurance commissioner can refer the matter to the state attorney general for criminal prosecution and possible imprisonment.

that are not "self-supporting". Interest rates used to determine non-guaranteed elements may not be greater than the earned interest rate underlying the insurer's disciplined current scale. (Disciplined current scale, a new term, means a scale that is reasonably based on actual recent historical experience, certified annually by the insurer's illustration actuary.)

The prospective insured must sign the illustration used during the presentation and copies must be provided to the insurer and the applicant. Even if no policy illustration is used, both the agent and the applicant must certify in writing to that effect.

The model also requires the insurance company to provide the policyholder with an annual report on the status of the policy, and notify the policyholder of any changes that would have a negative effect on policy values.

The new regulation is a first step toward requiring agents to use illustrations ethically and responsibly. Experts recommend using in-force illustrations at the annual policy review to continue explaining product performance and provide proper account servicing.

"The NAIC model is a partial fix of the problem," says Bill Free of the LUTC. "Mandatory in-force illustrations are another."

Disciplinary Actions

State laws differ on what constitutes grounds for denial, suspension, revocation, or nonrenewal of an insurance agent's license. In general, an agent can lose his or her license for violating any insurance laws, obtaining a license through misrepresentation or fraud, or for "lack of trustworthiness and competence", which is variously defined by state law and industry practice.

In most states, an agent's or broker's license may be revoked, suspended for up to 12 months, or license renewal may be refused for the following:

- ✔ Any cause for which the original license or any renewal would have been refused
- ✔ Willful violation of or noncompliance with any insurance statute, lawful rule or regulation

- ✔ Misrepresentation or fraud in obtaining or attempting to obtain an insurance license (such as cheating on the licensing exam)
- ✔ Misappropriation or conversion to personal use, or illegal withholding, of monies belonging to policyholders, insurers, beneficiaries or others and received during the conduct of insurance business
- ✔ Suspension or revocation of an insurance license in any jurisdiction
- ✔ Conviction by final judgment of a felony involving moral turpitude
- ✔ Conduct of insurance affairs showing the licensee to be incompetent or a source of injury and loss to, or repeated complaints by, the public or any insurer

The license of a firm or corporation also may be suspended, revoked or refused for cause if such cause applies to any individual designated in the license. The revocation or suspension of an agent or broker license will automatically revoke or suspend the licenses of all solicitors appointed by that agent or broker.

Most agent licenses are suspended or revoked based on fiduciary misconduct (especially commingling, misappropriation, or improper withholding of client funds, and failing to remit return premiums due), charging of additional fees, felony convictions, etc.

How Insurance Departments Find The Bad Guys

Patterns of agent misconduct may be uncovered during the course of market conduct examinations. Also, insurance departments have investigative units that follow up on complaints of wrongful conduct on the part of insurance agents. Insurance departments have the power to investigate, review, hold hearings, and, if necessary, suspend, nonrenew, or revoke the insurance agent's license and may impose civil penalties in the form of fines and jail sentences based on the violations uncovered.

How To Stay Out Of Trouble

Besides the obvious: adhering to state laws and abiding by

Common Agent Violations in Colorado

Stephen St.Cyr, CIE, the senior market conduct examiner for the Colorado Division of Insurance, reports that agent practices are looked at "to a moderate degree" during market conduct exams in his state. "The application process and upfront (field) underwriting are of the most interest," says St.Cyr. The most frequently uncovered agent violations in Colorado include placing business with an insurer before being appointed, policy cancellations which disregard statutory requirements, declining insurance applicants without legal basis, misquoting, and lack of full and fair disclosure. Penalties related to agent activities are most likely to occur in the risk selection/declination process, St.Cyr reports.

the Golden Rule, there are ways for agents to keep out of trouble. Compliance skills should be learned along with basic product knowledge and sales skills. Field offices and agencies may establish their own "code of ethics" to be used in the course of business. Agencies may conduct regular meetings for staff regarding market conduct and compliance. Agents can also take industry ethics courses to learn more about their legal and ethical responsibilities.

"I would advise agents to communicate frequently and thoroughly with their companies' compliance departments, underwriting, and claims departments," recommends Colorado's St.Cyr. "Direct contact with their divisions of insurance is also recommended."

Agents must take special care to follow strict procedures (and train all employees to do the same) in taking applications, placing coverages, explaining coverages, collecting premiums, submitting changes to policies upon an insured's request, and preparing claim forms. Any error or omission could result in losing a client and could lead to a lawsuit.

And there's plenty that can go wrong. Agents may find themselves in trouble because of a client's selective memory. For whatever reason, a client may decide he or she no longer needs or wants a policy purchased years ago, and may hope to get out of the contract by crying "misrepresentation".

An agent could be contacted by an attorney representing a client policyholder, who claims her life insurance policy was misrepresented as a retirement vehicle. They are threatening to file suit against the agent seeking damages, file complaints with the insurance department and the insurance carrier, and go after the agent's insurance license.

If the agent has not kept detailed notes, correspondence, etc. on the original transaction, the recommendations made, the client's acceptance/non-acceptance of those recommendations, etc., he or she may be at the mercy of the client's memory. The best way to protect against problems like this is by conducting needs-based selling, performing all the required disclosure at the time the sale is made, and most importantly, documenting everything. This advice becomes doubly important when replacing an existing life insurance policy.

Internal Compliance Audits

Just as insurance companies conduct their own internal audits of compliance, with the increasing regulation of agent activities it is a good idea for agents and agencies to conduct internal reviews as well.

Agents are encouraged to review their own agency practices, sales materials and sales practices, and determine whether they are in compliance both with state laws and home office guidelines. Agents should maintain a file of sales materials that are used and discard any older sales materials that may be out of compliance with current requirements. (Note, however, that anything that has been used as an advertisement or sales material may need to be retained for at least three years as part of state recordkeeping requirements.) Everything should be reviewed, from preapproach letters, advertisements, business cards, brochures, etc. to telephone presentations, data collection (fact finders), illustrations, policy descriptions, receipts, newsletters, annual policy reviews, and all correspondence with the applicant/policyholder.

Once the agent has identified which materials are out of compliance, he or she should take immediate steps to revise them. Identifying what is and what is not a fair sales practice these days can be difficult. What may previously have been considered a top sales approach may now have become grounds for termination of agent appointment. Agents can seek guidance from the home office on questionable materials, or may decide to use only materials from the insurer's list of approved sales materials.

Typical E&O Insurance Agreement

A sample E&O insuring agreement could look like this:

Coverage is provided for an act, error, or omission in rendering or failing to render professional services in the conduct of the named insured's profession as a licensed agent for life and health insurance.

USING E&O COVERAGE FOR PROTECTION

Because insurance agents have professional and fiduciary responsibilities to both insureds and insurers, they can be held legally liable for the consequences of any negligence or errors or omissions committed during the course of conducting their business.

An agent has a duty to evaluate a client's insurance needs and to make proper insurance recommendations. A failure to address an insurance need, or a recommendation that leaves a serious gap in coverage, could leave an insured with a loss that is not covered but should have been covered. In such cases, the insured may have a valid legal claim against the agent for damages.

If an agent carelessly and erroneously tells an insured that something is covered by a policy which actually excludes that kind of loss, and if the courts decide that a valid waiver by the agent created the coverage, the insurer could be held liable for any loss that occurs. Although the insurer might have to pay the insured, it could have a valid legal liability claim against the agent and could sue to recover whatever payment was made.

Smart agents keep files of client correspondence, signed

disclosure forms, etc., to help prove they have acted properly (if ever the need should arise). Without such documentation, it's the agent's word against the buyer's. Smart agents also carry errors and omissions protection. (Just one uninsured malpractice claim can put an agency out of business.) In fact, a few states have mandated that all agents carry E&O insurance, primarily for the protection of consumers.

Errors and omissions insurance is purchased as protection for professionals (such as insurance agents) who give advice to their clients. It provides indemnity for negligence, error, or omission by the insurer, or agent who is the insurer's representative. E&O policies protect agents from financial losses they may suffer if insureds sue to recover for their financial loss due to an agent giving them incorrect advice (error) or not informing them of an important issue (omission). This coverage would apply to negligence, errors and omissions, but not to intentional acts or fraud. Thus, an agent could not intentionally and knowingly exceed agency authority and hope to be protected by E&O coverage for any resulting liability.

Insurance agents may purchase an individual E&O policy, a policy through the agency, or through the insurance company. Although there are no standard "insurance agency" E&O policies, they do have certain basic characteristics in common. E&O policies usually have a high deductible, such as $1,000 or more, which may be tied to the number of agency employees. The coverage is usually written with a limit per claim, but aggregate limits for all claims during the policy period are also available. Common limits range from $100,000 to $2 million or more.

Except for obvious exclusions, (intentional acts, criminal acts, liability assumed under contract, bodily and personal injury) E&O policies have few other exclusions. However, some E&O coverages are beginning to exclude things like coverage for placing business with insurers who become insolvent.

Agents and agencies should review proposed E&O coverages as closely as they review coverages for a prospective insured with complex insurance needs. There are many choices available as to the policies themselves, as well as available endorsements, extensions of coverage, and coordination with other coverages (such as the agency's fidelity coverages). Shopping carefully will pay off not only in potential premiums savings but better coverage, as well.

Insurance agents today need the protection of E&O coverage because their business is complex and errors and omissions do occur. However, an agent's best line of defense against errors and omissions claims is to become as knowledgeable as possible about the insurance business and to always conduct business in an ethical and professional manner.

✔ Check Your Understanding

1. Stan submits an application for term life insurance with ABC Life Co. to his insurance agent Howie and pays the first annual premium. A few days later, Howie realizes Stan would be better off with the identical term policy offered by XYZ Life. He hasn't mailed in Stan's application yet, and knowing Stan is out of the country for a month, he just goes ahead and switches Stan over to the better deal. What potential problems could Howie encounter?

2. Leslie's agent prepares a policy illustration to show her what kind of return she might expect on the investment portion of her life insurance policy. What should her agent make her aware of when presenting the illustration?

3. Mrs. Harris has had her present life insurance policy for 19 years. Her agent suggests she should cash it in for a different policy. Why might this be a disadvantage for Mrs. Harris?

4. Bill works as an agent for the ABC Insurance Agency. Bill sold a commercial insurance policy to XYZ Plastics, Inc. but forget to ask the insurer to include an endorsement that he told XYZ would be included. Now, XYZ has had a loss that would have been covered if Bill had asked for the endorsement. What kind of coverage might be available to cover this loss?

5. Kate takes an application for health insurance from Everett, but Everett declines to pay the initial premium up front. Everett has indicated he is in excellent health on the application. But one month later, when Kate visits him to deliver the policy and collect the first premium, Everett is clearly in poor health. What are Kate's responsibilities?

CHAPTER 3

THE AGENT'S RESPONSIBILITIES TO THE INSURANCE COMPANY

Agents and insurers should work together to provide the best insurance products and services to consumers. In a perfect world, the interests of the insurance agent, insurance company, and insurance applicant/policyholder would all be in alignment. Unfortunately, such is not always the case.

Clearly, an agent's duties to the insurance carrier extend beyond the mere fulfillment of the strict terms in the agency agreement. As in all business dealings, the agent must:

- ✔ Display utmost good faith, honesty, and integrity in dealing with the carrier
- ✔ Follow the carrier's reasonable instructions (within the confines of the law)
- ✔ Avoid conflicts of interest in representing multiple carriers
- ✔ Solicit business that will be profitable both to the agent and the principal

With this in mind, as we discuss the agent's responsibilities to the carrier, we will omit commonsense directives such as "obey all relevant state laws" and "perform duties with reasonable skill and care", focusing instead on the agent's direct contractual and legal obligations to the principal.

Contractual Obligations

The agent's contract or agency agreement with the insurer will specify the agent's duties and responsibilities to the principal. The contract will identify the parties in the contract, the contract's expiration or renewal date,

$.32 vs. $500

State records are replete with examples of fines against agents for such "minor" infractions as failing to notify the department of insurance within 30 days of an address change.

Fines and penalties vary from state to state, but neglecting to spend 32 cents on a notification of address change can translate into:

- ✔ a $100 administrative fine and consent order in Nebraska
- ✔ a $500 fine and 60-day license suspension in Wisconsin

and the extent of the agent's authority.

In all insurance transactions, the agent's responsibility is to act in accordance with the agency contract and thus for the benefit of the insurer. If an agent violates the agency agreement, then he or she may be held personally liable to the insurer for breach of contract.

Reasonable Person Standard

An agent has a duty to act with a degree of care that a reasonable person would exercise under similar circumstances. This prudent person rule is to protect the insurer and the insured from unreasonable insurance transactions on the part of the agent.

Fiduciary Duty

The agent also has a fiduciary duty to the insurer, and must account for all property, including money, which comes into his or her possession. Agents who collect premiums from insureds are liable for transmitting those payments to the insurer. State statutes provide that payment to the agent or broker constitutes payment to the insurance company. The agent must not embezzle or commingle these funds.

Reporting Changes

Agents are often contractually required to report any changes of home or business address immediately to the carrier(s) with whom they hold an appointment, as well as to all regulatory authorities such as the state insurance department. Statutes usually specify this notice should be made "immediately," "within 30 days," or "within a reasonable time".

Maintaining E&O Coverage

Some agency contracts also now require that the agent obtain and maintain errors and omissions coverage. This protects the agent in case an agent error causes losses for the insurance company, and the company sues the agent for recovery.

Formation of an Insurance Contract

Understanding how insurance policy contracts are formed is essential to understanding the agent's responsibilities to the insurance company. The insurance contract is a legal document which is subject to the general law of contracts, a distinct body of law which is separate from criminal law (crimes against society) and tort law (legal liability usually involving damages for negligence).

The insurance contract defines the parties to the contract, establishes the intent of the parties, and details the exact responsibilities of each party. A simplified explanation of the insuring agreement would be: The insurer promises to pay the insured according to the terms of the policy if a loss occurs.

It is very important for an agent to understand the limitations of the contract and to operate within its limits. To do otherwise could place the agent in a position of personal liability.

Elements of a Contract

For any contract to be binding, there must be **competent parties**. That is, all parties must have the legal capacity to make a contract.

To have the legal capacity to make insurance contracts, an insurance company must have authority under its charter to issue contracts and be authorized by the state to issue contracts. Similarly, the agent must be licensed by the state. The legal effect of a contract made by an unlicensed insurer or unlicensed agent depends on state law.

The insured or applicant must be of **legal age** and be **mentally competent** to make an insurance contract. Applications of minors must usually be signed by an adult parent or guardian to comply with the legal age requirement for making contracts. To be valid, a contract must be for a **legal purpose** and not contrary to public policy.

Each party to the contract must give valuable **consideration**. In the insurance contract, the value given by the insurer consists of the promises contained in the policy contract. The consideration given by the insured consists of the statements made in the application and the payment of the initial premium.

Property & Casualty Insurance

In property and casualty insurance, the prospect who applies

Agents and Risk Selection

In accordance with agency law, information given to the agent is the same as providing the information to the insurer.

If the agent knows of anything adverse concerning the risk to be insured, it is his or her responsibility to provide this information to the insurer. To withhold important underwriting information could harm the insurer's risk selection process.

It is also important for the agent to know each represented carrier's underwriting guidelines before soliciting business.

for insurance usually makes the initial offer. An agent may accept immediately by issuing an oral or written binder, or the application may be sent to an insurer and acceptance may depend upon an inspection or additional information. An insurer or agent may also make the initial offer, by soliciting insurance business. In any event, one party must offer and the other must accept before a binding agreement exists.

Advice to Agents: Err on the Side of Full Disclosure

State law usually requires the agent and the applicant to certify in writing that the applicant has read, or had read to him, the completed application and that the applicant realizes that any false statement or misrepresentation may result in loss of coverage.

Failure to complete an application accurately and honestly could subject the agent to disciplinary action both by the company and the insurance department.

Life & Health Insurance

The formation of a life or health insurance contract is somewhat different in that the life or health agent usually does not have the authority to put a policy into effect. The agent can only solicit offers from prospective insureds, securing their applications and initial premium payments. The insurance company approves and issues the contract after receiving the application and premium from the agent.

The restricted underwriting authority of the life insurance agent is related to the nature of life insurance contracts. The insurance company is in a much better position than the agent to evaluate the applicant's insurability.

Life insurance policies are generally non-cancellable, long-term contracts. A life insurance policy is contestable only for a one or two-year period. Property and casualty insurance, by comparison, involves a short-term contract often for one year or less and the insurance company usually reserves the right to cancel the policy if the risk appears to be undesirable. In addition, life and health insurance underwriting decisions frequently rest on medical questions. The life or health insurer employs medical experts and has at its disposal various investigative reports that shed light on the desirability of a risk.

Field Underwriting

By definition, underwriting is the process of selection, classification and rating of risks. During the risk selection process information is evaluated to determine whether the risk is acceptable, and how the individual or risk will be classified (preferred, standard or substandard). Once this part of the underwriting procedure is complete, the policy will be rated in terms of the premium which the applicant will pay. The policy will then be issued and subsequently delivered by the agent.

In many insurance sales, the agent is the primary collector of underwriting information. A primary objective of the agent as a field underwriter is to help protect the insurance company from **adverse selection**. When confronted with an impaired risk, it is up to the agent to ask the right questions and submit the proper information to the underwriting department so the appropriate policy can be issued.

By fully explaining the applicant's medical conditions (course of treatment, present status) or hazardous activities (mountain climbing, aviation, etc.) the agent may be able to avoid underwriting declinations. When an applicant is found to be a substantial risk, the agent is responsible for delivering the policy as issued and explaining its limitations and/or extra premium to the applicant.

The Application Process

It is the agent's responsibility to obtain necessary information from the insurance applicant and to accurately complete the application for insurance and to ensure that all the proper signatures have been obtained. Much of the information reported on the application becomes the basis upon which to accept or reject the proposed insured. A signed and witnessed copy of the application becomes part of the legal contract of insurance between the insured and the insurer and thus it is critical that the application be accurate.

Typically, the application asks for the following information:

- ✔ Applicant's name and address
- ✔ Type of insurance requested
- ✔ Property/hazard to be insured
- ✔ Location and description of property to be insured
- ✔ Prior loss experience
- ✔ Any known hazards
- ✔ Background information on the applicant
- ✔ Limits of insurance requested

Applications for life and health insurance generally require detailed information regarding the insured's past medical history, current physical condition and personal morals. Many times, the proposed insured must undergo a medical examination.

In health insurance, field underwriting is even more impor-

Signing Someone Else's Name is Always Forgery

- ✔ An agent in Pennsylvania signed an insured's name to a disability waiver, resulting in a $1,000 civil penalty and three years of license supervision.
- ✔ A Wisconsin agent found signing documents without the proper authority received a $500 fine and a 60-day license suspension.
- ✔ A New York agent signed the insured's name on a change of broker request form without the individual's consent, resulting in a $500 fine.
- ✔ An Ohio agent who completed an insurance application without the insured's knowledge or permission was compelled to surrender his license voluntarily.

Important Fraud Definitions

A **misrepresentation** is a written or oral statement which is false. Generally, in order for a misrepresentation to be grounds for voiding an insurance policy, it has to be **material** to the risk.

Material information is that which if the insurance company had known the correct information at the time of application, the application would have been denied, or issued in a different manner. An example would be concealing prior loss experiences to help reduce premiums.

Concealment is the failure to disclose known facts.

Fraud is an intentional act designed to deceive and induce another party to part with something of value. Fraud may involve misrepresentation and concealment but not all acts of misrepresentation and concealment are acts of fraud.

tant than in life insurance. **Moral risk** is a heavy factor in health insurance underwriting because of the possibility of malingering, and it is the agent, not the home office underwriter, who has personal contact with the applicant. **Moral risk** or **moral hazard** refers to the assessment of an applicant's habits, lifestyle, financial responsibility, environment, character and general reputation. These are taken into account when underwriting life and health insurance to determine if the applicant presents a standard insurable risk.

Moral hazards usually arise from a combination of weak conscience and financial difficulty. An example would be a person's willingness to pad medical expenses or to extend disability leave unnecessarily (malingering).

It is the responsibility of the agent to be sure to ask the applicant medical and nonmedical questions clearly and precisely and to record the answers the same way. The agent must be careful to present the facts and not his or her interpretation of the facts. If the agent has any suspicions whatsoever, he or she should probe when taking the application, or, if the matter is not one he or she can probe, any suspicions should be stated to the underwriting department in the space provided on most applications for agent's comments. The goals of the agent are to get complete and accurate information from the applicant and to detect the possibility of moral hazard.

As a field underwriter, the agent can help expedite the underwriting process by the prompt submission of the application. The sooner the application is forwarded, the sooner the policy can be issued. But agents get in trouble for failing to submit applications in a timely manner all the time. The agent may also help by scheduling the applicant for a physical exam (if necessary) and by assisting the home office underwriter with other requirements such as obtaining an Attending Physician's Statement.

A signed and witnessed copy of the application becomes part of the legal contract of insurance between the insured and the insurer, so it is of utmost importance that the application information be accurate and complete, and that the proper signatures are secured. A commonly cited market conduct violation is the agent's failure to accurately disclose information submitted on the insurance applications. More importantly, material omissions or errors might subject the applicant to denial of benefits, voiding of the policy, and even prosecution for fraud.

The **Agent's Statement** is part of the application and requires that the agent provide certain information regarding the proposed insured. Generally, this includes information regarding the agent's relationship to the insured, data about the proposed insured's financial status, habits, general character and any other information which may be pertinent to the risk being assumed by the insurer.

Applications and Fraud

Fraud can be committed:

- ✔ By the applicant without the agent's knowledge,
- ✔ By the agent without the applicant's knowledge, or
- ✔ By both working in conjunction.

Agents have advised applicants to omit information to ensure the applicant will be issued coverage, or will be issued coverage at a lower premium. Sometimes agents illegally sign applications on behalf of the applicant, in the belief they are helping the client expedite the request for coverage.

Under current practice, if an agent enhances a life insurance applicant's occupation on the application in order to help the applicant get a lower premium, and the policy is issued, if a claim occurs during the first two policy years the insurance company may deny the claim based on misrepresentation. Whether this seems fair or not may depend on whether the applicant co-conspired to adjust the application in order to reduce his or her own premium.

The carrier has entrusted the agent to collect all the information relevant to accepting or declining a risk. If pertinent facts are concealed, omitted, or understated, the insurer may take on risks it would not otherwise accept, or may collect insufficient premium for the risk.

Other Field Underwriting Issues

Company underwriters are increasingly relying on paramedical exams and blood tests for information in order to accurately evaluate life and health risks. Blood testing is almost universally used to determine cholesterol levels, elevated liver enzymes, and the presence of HIV infection. In many jurisdictions, HIV testing requires informed consent of the applicant, condfidentiality of results, and proper notification procedures.

Advice to Agents: Never Accept Cash

Agents should adopt a policy of **never** accepting cash payments from insureds.

Cash makes the recordkeeping function more complicated, makes commingling of funds too tempting, and opens the agent up to claims of wrongdoing if the insured asserts he or she paid the agent more than they actually did.

It is safest to accept premium payments as checks made out to the issuing company.

Application-Related Violations

- ✔ Knowingly and willfully made or permitted a false or fraudulent statement on an insurance policy application (Nebraska - $300 fine)
- ✔ Misrepresented terms of a proposed insurance contract (Nebraska - $300 fine)
- ✔ Knowingly and willfully made a misrepresentation relative to an application for insurance (Nebraska - $500 fine)
- ✔ Submitted an application for automobile insurance that contained fraudulent driver information (New York - license revoked)
- ✔ Misrepresented information pertaining to a driver's history and auto accidents resulting in lower premiums being charged (Pennsylvania - $1,000 penalty, 5-year license supervision)
- ✔ Falsified application in order to avoid a higher rate (Pennsylvania - $500 penalty, 3-year future supevision)

A controversial field underwriting issue has arisen in long term care insurance, where effective underwriting is the key to profitability. Along with questions about the applicant's physical health, questions about cognitive functions, mental health, and lifestyle evaluations are increasingly being made part of the underwriting function.

A large percentage of long term care carriers report using a variety of screening methods, including the telephone interview, attending physicians' statements, face-to-face interviews, etc. Applications and paramedical exams incorporate cognitive assessments, and in many cases the agent is relied upon for specific input.

Collection of Premium

Agents frequently **collect premiums** from insureds and applicants, and **receive return premiums** from insurers. It is the agent's duty to make certain that these premiums are submitted to the appropriate party promptly. All insurance-related funds received by an agent are received in a **fiduciary** capacity and must be held in trust. An agent may establish separate accounts for fiduciary funds, or may deposit all such funds in a single account — in either case the agent's records must clearly distinguish the amount of funds held for each person.

The agent must account for and pay the correct amounts to insureds, insurers, and others who are entitled to the money. These funds should not be mixed with personal funds. Mixing personal funds with the insured or insurer's funds is an illegal practice known as **commingling**.

Any agent who takes funds held in trust and puts those funds to personal use is guilty of theft or misuse of funds and will be punished as provided by law. Usually a misuse of funds is punishable by suspension or revocation of license, and fines may also be imposed.

Ultimately, an agent must **remit all premiums** received to the insurer or insurers entitled to the funds. Since it would not be convenient for the agent or the insurer to transfer funds on every business transaction, money is accumulated and periodically transferred. Generally, funds are remitted according to some variation of monthly accounting. Some agents may remit funds based on payments received during the month, while others may remit funds based on amounts billed to insureds during the month.

Submitting the Application & Initial Premium

It is important for the agent to submit the application, initial premium, and any questionnaires or other forms to the home office underwriter promptly. The agent should review all forms for completeness and be sure that they are properly signed. Not only does this make for good relationships with the home office underwriter, but it is extremely important to the applicant. Unnecessary delays in delivering the policy can cause the applicant undue anxiety and result in a loss of confidence in the agent. Since agents are handling money belonging to their clients, it is extremely important that an accurate record of such transactions be kept. It is also wise for the agent to keep copies of applications and other information. This avoids unnecessary delay or other problems if the originals are lost.

When the initial premium is **not paid** with a health insurance application some insurers require that the agent send a transmittal notice verifying the date he or she received the first premium. Also, because the policy is not effective until the first premium has been paid and the policy has been delivered, the agent must get a statement at the time the policy is delivered. This statement verifies, basically, two things; one, that the insured has not suffered injury or illness since the time of the application to the date of policy delivery, and two, that the insured has not seen a physician with regard to any interim injury or illness.

Policy Delivery

Since policy delivery is necessary to complete the sale of an insurance policy, the best way to assure delivery is to do it in person. If a conditional receipt has not been previously issued, the insurer may require the agent to obtain a statement of good health at the time of policy delivery.

Although most policies contain a provision barring an agent from changing the policy contract in any way, the company may be liable for errors made by the agent if the agent incorrectly represents the policy being sold. If the policy has been issued with any changes or amendments, the agent will also

When Fraud is Suspected

Studies show that even individuals who generally consider themselves to be "honest" think there is nothing wrong with inflating insurance claims in order to collect more than they would otherwise be entitled to after a loss has occured.

One of the most difficult decisions an agent may have to make is when he or she suspects a valued client of submitting a fraudulent or exaggerated claim.

Conversely, the agent must be careful not to charge someone with fraud when there is no evidence of fraudulent activities.

More Application Violations

- ✔ An Ohio agent was convicted of petty theft, a first degree misdemeanor, for taking an application, failing to submit it to the insurance company, and failing to inform the insured that no coverage was in effect.
- ✔ In Vermont, a consumer paid $9,300 to Hall Insurance Agency to purchase workers compensation in January of 1993. The application was rejected because the agency check to the carrier bounced. For a year, the client was unaware that no coverage was in effect. The agency's and agent's license were suspended.
- ✔ In Wisconsin, an agent was ordered to pay a $5,000 fine, make restitution of $10,000, and had his insurance license revoked for failing to submit applications to the insurer and converting premiums to his own use.
- ✔ In another Wisconsin case, an agent who failed to submit applications to the insurer was compelled to surrender his license and agreed not to apply for an insurance license in the future.

be required to explain these changes and obtain the insured's signature acknowledging receipt of these amendments, and forward the signed statement to the home office.

Conditional Receipt

Agents may give the applicant a **conditional receipt** if the premium is paid at the time of the application. This receipt makes the coverage effective on the date of the application, if the applicant is found to be insurable under the company's general underwriting rules in effect at the time of application. However, some conditional receipts make coverage effective on the date of application, or the date of the medical examination, whichever is later.

For example, an applicant has paid the initial premium, completed and signed the application. The agent provides the applicant with a conditional receipt which basically states that the applicant is covered as of the date of the application (or receipt) provided he or she is insurable as a standard risk. Thus, if the applicant were to die before the policy was issued, the beneficiary would receive the face amount of the policy.

On the other hand, if the applicant was found to be a substandard risk, then the conditional receipt is null and void and no coverage would be effective until the substandard policy was delivered and additional premium paid. If the policy is not issued as applied for (a substandard rating, for example), then no coverage would be in force until the applicant accepts the substandard policy and pays the additional premium required by the rating.

Binding Receipt

A few companies authorize agents to issue an "unconditional" or **binding receipt** that makes the company liable for the risk from the date of application. This coverage lasts for a specified time or until the insurer either issues a policy or declines the application, if earlier. The specified time limit is usually 30 to 60 days.

With a binding receipt, regardless of the applicant's insurability, he or she is covered for a specific period of time following completion of the application and the payment of the initial premium. Use of this type of receipt for life and health policies is rare.

Controlled Business

When an agent becomes licensed, he or she must intend to actively engage in the insurance business with members of the public, and not use the license principally for transacting a disproportionate amount of **controlled business**. Controlled business means insurance on the agent's, broker's, or solicitor's own property or interests, or those of his family, his employer, or any partnership, association, or corporation in which he or a family member has an interest as an officer, director, stockholder, partner or employee.

A certain amount of controlled business is permitted (and this amount differs from state to state). But a licensee may not be permitted to earn commission or compensation from controlled business in excess of a stated amount (10% to 50% of total compensation, depending upon the state) during a stated time period (usually a calendar year). If a greater proportion does come from controlled business, the practice is in violation of law and the producer's license may be revoked or suspended.

Reviewing Agent Files

"One thing I've noticed recently is an increase in the number of actual on-site visits to agent offices to conduct interviews and review files in conjunction with market conduct examinations," reports a representative from the NAIC.

In fact, one relatively common agent-related market conduct citation involves "failure to respond to the department's inquiries."

Claims Handling

Regardless of the type of insurance, the insurer will usually require a written notice of loss or claim and supporting documents. Notice of loss provided to the insurance agent is considered notice to the carrier, so the agent is responsible for transmitting notice to the carrier as quickly as possible.

As mentioned in the previous chapter, agents should be careful of assuring the policyholder that the loss will be covered unless they are absolutely sure the circumstances of the loss are within the policy's scope of coverage. Agents should not provide legal advice, or make unauthorized decisions on behalf of the insurance company.

Claims and Fraud

Agents must be particularly alert to consumer fraud at claims time; any evidence of:

- ✔ Fraudulent claims
- ✔ Exaggerated claims, or
- ✔ Malingering

should be reported to the carrier immediately. Examples of fraudulent claims include:

- ✔ Resisting the return to work after a disability, claiming an illness or injury is persisting when in fact it is not
- ✔ Claiming an injury that occurred at home as a work-related injury in order to collect workers compensation benefits
- ✔ Arson
- ✔ Adding to a list of stolen property items that were not stolen, or inflating the value of items that were stolen
- ✔ Including preexisting damage (fender scratches, etc.) to the reported loss

Fraudulent claims are investigated at both the state and company level. Many state insurance departments have established fraud investigation units and impose heavy fines and penalties for those caught submitting fraudulent claims. Likewise, the larger insurance companies have special investigative units (SIUs) to conduct claims reviews and to help detect and prevent fraudulent claims.

Falsifying Applications

A West Virginia insurance agent was discovered selling life policies to people age 68 and over, and backdating the birth year on their applications by 10 years. Thinking the applicant younger and more insurable, the insurance company issued the policies without question — until the first death claim. Benefits were denied based on material misrepresentation.

"This guy sold 20 or 30 policies like this before he was caught," says John Davidson, director of consumer services. After investigating and finding that the agent had acted alone without the knowledge of the applicants, the department of insurance ordered the death claim paid. The insurer fired the agent, cancelled the other policies, and returned the premiums paid. The agent's license was subsequently revoked.

Reporting Misconduct

Another area of agent responsibility that has surfaced in recent years is a clause in either the agency contract or the insurer's compliance manual asking the agent to report suspected or confirmed misconduct on the part of other agents or company employees. This has come about because many times agents are aware that their colleagues are violating fair practices laws before the insurance company uncovers the behavior. Company compliance officers now hold everyone in the company responsible for monitoring compliance.

Agent's Office and Records

The insurance agent represents the carrier in maintaining complete policyholder records. But keeping accurate records is more than a service to the insurance company; it is essential for the agent to protect himself or herself.

State laws require agents and brokers to have and maintain in the state issuing the license a place of business accessible to the public, where the licensee principally conducts transactions under the license. Licenses must be conspicuously displayed in a part of the place of business open to the public.

The agent or broker must keep at the principal place of business all records concerning transactions conducted under the insurance license. Required information includes a record of each policy sold, name and address of insured, the policy number and term, and the general nature of the subject of insurance. Other records that the agent is generally responsible for maintaining include:

- ✔ Applications, premium, and production records, coverage and correspondence from the date of application or policy delivery
- ✔ Any written agreements used for the charging of fees (like consulting fees) outside of the policy or contract terms
- ✔ Detailed bank records (account statements, deposit records, cancelled checks and withdrawal records)
- ✔ Written disclosure statements

Records must usually be kept for a minimum period of time (such as three years or five years), and must be made available for examination in the event they are requested by the insurance department.

Policy Retention

Although much of the business of the agent is involved in attracting potential clients, retaining the account and servicing it through the years is important as well — both to the agent and the insurance carrier.

The agent becomes involved with the client and the client's family after original application and delivery, at times of change, such as when the client gets married, has a child, purchases new property, or dies. The agent acts as the representative of the company in changing beneficiaries, adding amounts of insurance, and facilitating payment of claims.

Penalties for Moving Records Out of State

A Texas agency that moved its books and records out of state without the permission of the Texas Department of Insurance was fined $6,250. A Texas company that committed the same violation received a $15,000 fine.

Recordkeeping Violations

Disciplinary actions can be taken against agents for poor recordkeeping or other recordkeeping violations. From the state case files:

- ✔ Made false entries pertaining to an insured so as to reflect inaccurate bookkeeping (Nebraska - $1,000 administrative fine)
- ✔ Failed to maintain proper records of insurance business (New York - license revoked)
- ✔ Failure to maintain policyholder records as required causing a delay in submitting a disability application (Wisconsin - $500 fine and cease and desist agreement)

"Good, solid, long standing client relationships are the best possible result," says one industry expert. "They're good for business, they're good for agents, and they're good for consumers." The effectiveness of the agent at these times will lead to retention of the account for the lifetime of the client, and often over generations.

✔ Check Your Understanding

1. Why does the home office retain more of the underwriting responsibility when it comes to life and health insurance?

2. John puts all of his premiums and other operating income in his agency's checking account. Could this be a problem?

3. Susan's agency has a number of people who come to her office and pay their insurance premiums in cash. One day Susan receives a call from a policyholder who claims she paid her full year's premium in cash six months ago but just received a semi annual bill. What would you recommend Susan do?

4. Mike got an insurance agent's license so he can help the members of his large family find the best deals on auto insurance coverage. Are there any regulations he should be aware of in doing this?

____

____

____

____

____

____

5. Bob likes to sell insurance but occasionally forgets to keep records on all his clients. Without complete and accurate records, what kinds of problems could he encounter?

____

____

____

____

____

____

CHAPTER 4

THE INSURER'S RESPONSIBILITIES TO POLICYHOLDERS

As providers of a broad range of products which perform a variety of important social and economic functions, insurers are valued both as employers and responsible corporate citizens.

An insurer's reputation is one of its greatest strengths, and high ethical standards are the cornerstone of that reputation. Each insurance company should attempt to meet its obligations in an ethical manner which earns the respect of policyowners, clients, regulators, employees, business associates, and the community. The insurer's employees and agents contribute to the high ethical standards of the company and continue to enhance its reputation and image.

To accomplish these goals, the insurer attempts to:

- ✔ Conduct its business in a fair, lawful, and ethical manner
- ✔ Offer customers those products and services which are appropriate to their needs and provide fair value
- ✔ Maintain a climate which encourages agents and employees to be honest and fair in the conduct of their duties

A discussion of an insurance company's market responsibilities to policyholders could easily fill an entire volume. Naturally, policyholders may expect the insurer to comply with those laws and regulations pertaining to policyholder service such as fair sales and marketing practices, fair underwriting practices, fair claims practices, and fair notice of policy cancellations and nonrenewals.

Penalties in Colorado

"Any amount of fine has to do with the type and severity of the violation and whether it's an honest mistake or constitutes a pattern or practice in violation of Colorado statutes," explains Colorado Deputy Commissioner Maryellen Waggoner.

"Our largest fine ever in Colorado was $38,000 imposed in 1995 against State Farm."

Penalties usually result in a stipulated agreement with the company.

Policyholders also have the right to expect the insurer to comply with broader insurance laws, since ultimately violations of these laws result in some impact on the public. For example, an insurer that fails to maintain adequate reserves and becomes insolvent will be unable to fulfill its obligations to policyholders.

If agents are to conduct their business in an ethical manner, then the insurers must adhere to ethical principles and encourage similar conduct from their field force. Not only do the insurers have an ethical obligation to their agents but they also have such a responsibility to the general public as well. It is the duty of the insurer to make certain that its field force obeys the unfair marketing practices laws, such as misrepresentation, rebating, and twisting. It is equally important for the insurer to see to it that its claims personnel comply with the laws regarding claims settlements.

In short, it is important for the insurer to lead by example. If it doesn't, it will be difficult for the field force to perform their duties in an ethical manner. The insurer must enforce those laws which are pertinent to agent conduct and behavior as well as comply with the laws which apply to the functions of the insurer itself.

Most insurance companies have entire divisions devoted to compliance and are (or should be) well aware of their obligations towards policyholders. Insurer responsibilities are of utmost importance for the agent to understand, so that he or she can provide accurate advice to policyholders on what to expect from the insurance company (especially at claims time, when policyholders have lots of questions). Also, by knowing what to expect from the insurer, the agent can see to it that the company indeed follows through.

Insurers and Market Conduct

Market conduct examiners concentrate on an insurer's general business practices (rather than random violations or isolated incidents of misconduct) when determining whether a company is in violation of fair practices regulations. Any pattern that seems to indicate that a violation is a "general business practice" will likely result in sanctions and penalties, as will evidence of "systematic wrongdoing" by a company.

Industry analyst Joseph Belth (editor of the newsletter *Insurance Forum*) defines systematic wrongdoing as what occurs when an insurance company "creates an environment conducive to deception by:

- ✔ (1) utilizing commission structures or other incentives that encourage representatives to engage in deception
- ✔ (2) preparing or allowing the preparation of sales illustrations or other promotional materials that incorporate deception
- ✔ (3) condoning deception by overlooking rather than punishing representatives for its use
- ✔ (4) failing to disclose material information to policyowners and prospective policyowners."

Sales and Marketing

Sales and marketing are perhaps the most important functions in which the insurer must demonstrate its ethical and fiduciary responsibility toward the public. Generally, the purpose of state laws governing advertising and sales literature is to provide full and fair disclosure of all material information. Advertising information must not be obscure, ambiguous, deceptive, or misleading. All advertisements must be truthful and accurate.

Most of the recent attention to market conduct has stemmed from sales and marketing practices which were deemed unfair. The record setting $35 million fine against Prudential in 1996 stemmed in part from the company's failure "to responsibly monitor and discipline its agents for improper sales activities."

One problem is that home office personnel who develop and/or approve insurance policy language very often have no idea how the product will be sold. A policy that meets all the regulatory criteria may be sold in a completely misleading way, so it is important for the company to control the entire product development, marketing, and sales process in order to ensure compliance.

Generally, states require that advertising and sales material may not omit information or use statements which are misleading to potential buyers. Advertisements cannot use jargon or terminology that would be confusing for a person not knowledgeable about insurance coverages. An advertise-

Sworn Depositions Required in NY

In 1994, the New York Insurance Commissioner ordered the CEOs of all life insurance companies licensed in New York to review their advertising files and practices, determine compliance, and verify (by sworn deposition) that they were up to code.

The insurers were reminded that "All advertising, regardless of its origin, is the responsibility of the insurer whose policies are so advertised." Practices originating with or used by agents merely demonstrated "an inadequate control by the company over the content, form, and method of distribution of its advertisements." Companies were also encouraged to establish clear lines of communication, control, and responsibility over the dissemination of advertising and promotional materials and a procedure for centralizing the ultimate approval of all such advertising with company officials whose compensation is not linked to sales.

Deceptive Auto Insurance

A California carrier was fined $360,000 for deceptively marketing auto insurance policies as "financial responsibility bonds".

The company in effect avoided market regulations (such as DOI approval of rates and forms and the requirement to offer a good driver discount) by classifying the policies as surety bonds and not insurance.

In addition to the fine, the company agreed to discontinue the program and comply with specific reporting requirements of the Department of Insurance.

ment cannot use language which exaggerates benefits or fails to disclose policy exclusions or limitations.

It is common for insurance companies to use the services of celebrities and other prominent people for advertising purposes. Testimonials used in advertising must be applicable to the policy advertised and be given accurately. Such testimonials must indicate if the person giving the testimonial is being compensated or if the individual has any financial interest in the company.

Other ethical advertising standards include the following:

- ✔ It is misleading for an advertisement to imply or state that an insurer or a policy has been approved or endorsed by an individual or a group, unless it is in fact true
- ✔ Statistical information used in advertising must be accurate and reflect all material facts. Usually, the source of the statistical information must be disclosed.
- ✔ It is considered unethical and misleading if advertisements mislead the public with regard to the purpose of the policy, benefits to be derived from the policy or falsely identifying the type of policy being advertised. For example, it is unethical to deliberately refer to a life insurance policy which has the primary purpose of providing a death benefit as an investment product which will provide an investment return.
- ✔ Life insurance advertising may not imply or state that policy dividends are guaranteed. Nor may any sales literature or proposals combine guaranteed policy values (such as the cash value) with dividends which are not guaranteed.

Nationwide's "Show Cause" Order

In April 1996, Nationwide Insurance was issued a "show cause" order by the Florida Insurance Department alleging unethical marketing practices having to do with auto and homeowners policies, including evidence that the company coerces agents to engage in improper practices and pressures agents to sell unnecessary policies to consumers.

Nationwide maintains that it has a firm policy for strict

compliance with the laws and regulations in all states where it does business, and is contesting the Florida order.

Many states require the company to keep a file of advertisements used in the state; this would include advertisements used by agents. An interesting question arises with regard to independent agents who represent several companies and advertise under their own names. Who is held responsible for fair advertising depends on what types of products are being advertised and how much business is written with the principal.

Privacy, Disclosure & Fair Reporting

The insurance industry is one of the largest collectors and users of personal information. Two federal laws governing the disclosure and use of such personal information are the Fair Credit Reporting Act and the Privacy Act of 1974. The NAIC Model Privacy Act has also had an important impact by helping individual states to enact regulations governing privacy. These Acts protect individuals from misuse of personal information that has been collected about them, prohibit the use of deceptive practices in gathering such information, provide for advance notice to the individual when such information is to be collected, and provide guidelines for correcting inaccurate or otherwise disputed personal information.

Fair Credit Reporting Act

When an application is submitted to an insurance company, a consumer reporting agency may be used to obtain personal information about the applicant to be used in the underwriting evaluation. To protect the consumer's right to privacy in this situation, the federal Fair Credit Reporting Act includes procedures for consumer reporting agencies to follow in their dealings with businesses to ensure that records are confidential, accurate, relevant and properly used.

Consumer Reports. Consumer reports include written, oral and other forms of communication which a consumer reporting agency has regarding a consumer's credit, character, reputation, or habits, which is used or collected to determine whether or not a consumer is eligible for credit, insurance, employment or other purposes authorized under the Act. Consumer reports may only be issued to persons who have a legitimate business need for the information. Governmental agencies may also be provided with a consumer's name, present and former addresses, and present and past places of employment.

Investigative Consumer Reports. An investigative consumer report includes information on a consumer's character, general reputation, personal habits, and mode of living that is obtained through investigation, i.e., interviews with associates and friends and neighbors of the consumer.

Penalties

Failure to comply with the provisions of the Fair Credit Reporting Act makes the guilty party liable to the consumer for the sum of actual damages sustained as a result of the noncompliance; punitive damages deemed proper by a court; and the costs of an action which enforces liability, plus reasonable attorney's fees.

When the noncompliance is due to negligence, the guilty party must pay the consumer the sum of the consumer's actual damages, the costs of any successful action to enforce liability, plus reasonable attorney's fees.

Such reports may not be made unless the consumer is clearly and accurately notified in advance about the report in writing within three days of the date on which the report was first requested. The consumer must also be notified that he or she is allowed to request additional information.

Pretext Interviews. A pretext interview is an interview whereby a person, in an attempt to obtain information about another person, pretends to be someone he or she is not, misrepresents the true purpose of the interview, or refuses to properly identify him or herself. Generally, pretext interviews are prohibited. However, they may be conducted when there is evidence of criminal activity, fraud or misrepresentation.

Consumer Reporting Agencies. Consumer reporting agencies collect information on individuals, prepare reports, and make the reports available to persons or organizations having a legitimate reason to receive such information. These agencies may operate for profit; for example, a credit union. Or, agencies may be nonprofit, such as the Medical Information Bureau (MIB) which is a clearinghouse for confidential medical information on applicants for life insurance.

Prohibited Information. Consumer reporting agencies are specifically prevented from putting information in their reports about bankruptcies over 14 years old; suits and judgments over seven years old or in which the statute of limitations has expired, whichever period is longer; paid tax liens or accounts placed for collection or charged to profit which are over seven years old; arrests, indictments, or conviction of crime reports; and any other adverse information which took place seven years prior to the report. (These restrictions don't apply when the consumer credit report is used in connection with a credit transaction of $50,000 or more, a life insurance policy of $50,000 or more, or when it concerns employment of an individual earning $20,000 or more.)

Consumers' Rights. Consumers who feel that information in their files is inaccurate or incomplete may inform the consumer reporting agency, which then must reinvestigate and record its findings in a reasonable period of time. If the information is no longer accurate or verifiable, it must be deleted. If the dispute is not resolved after reinvestigation, the consumer may file a brief statement (not more than 100 words) concerning the problem, which then must be noted in any future consumer reports the agency provides on that consumer.

If insurance is denied, or charges are increased, based on information contained in a consumer report, the insurer must notify the consumer and report the name and address of the consumer reporting agency which made the report. If insurance is denied, or charges are increased, due to information obtained from a person or organization other than a consumer reporting agency, the insurer must disclose the nature of that information to the consumer upon request. The insurer is responsible for informing consumers of their right to request this information when the adverse action is communicated (at the time the person is either declined for insurance or is "rated up").

The maximum penalty for obtaining consumer information reports under false pretenses is $5,000, or imprisonment for one year, or both. The same penalty is imposed on officers or employees of consumer reporting agencies who have knowingly and willfully provided consumer information to a person not authorized to receive it.

Privacy Act of 1974

It became clear in the 1970s that with the vast numbers of organizations collecting and using personal information, controls were necessary to protect the public from inaccurate, or misused information. The Privacy Act of 1974 was designed to:

- ✔ Minimize intrusiveness
- ✔ Require fair and impartial collection, analysis, and presentation of information and reports
- ✔ Assure the public they can expect personal information to be handled in confidence

Disclosure Authorization. Applicants for insurance must be given advance notice of the insurer's practices regarding collection and use of personal information. Notice must be given promptly and in writing. Notice should be given in the following cases and in the following manner:

- ✔ If a third party is interviewed, the applicant must be given notice when the collection of information has begun
- ✔ If only the applicant is interviewed, the applicant must be given notice when the policy is delivered

Penalties

The commissioner of insurance has the authority to investigate any insurer, or any agency used by the insurer to collect information, to determine if the company is in compliance with insurance laws. If the commissioner believes that a violation of the Act has taken place he or she can conduct a hearing to determine the facts.

If a violation is found, the commissioner can issue a cease and desist order, but if the violator continues in violation, the commissioner can institute a fine of up to $10,000 for each violation. If the violation is one that happens with such frequency that it appears to be a general business practice, the fine for each violation can be up to $50,000.

Individual Privacy Rights

The NAIC Model Privacy Act also provides for the enforcement of individual rights. The individual has the right to information concerning himself or herself, and the right to correct inaccurate information, the right to know the reasons for being turned down for insurance, or any other adverse underwriting decision. These rights are those found under the Fair Credit Reporting Act.

A fine of $10,000, or up to one year in jail is the penalty for any person who obtains information that he or she has no legitimate reason to receive.

- ✔ If a policy is being renewed, the insured must be given notice by the renewal date
- ✔ If a policy is being reinstated, the applicant-insured must be given notice at the time the request is made
- ✔ If an insured is requesting a change in benefits, the insured must receive notice at the time the request is made

The notice must give the applicant or insured the following kinds of information:

- ✔ The people with access to personal information
- ✔ The kind of information to be collected
- ✔ The kind of information the insurer can receive without the applicant's prior approval
- ✔ The sources of information
- ✔ The persons to whom information may be disclosed without the applicant's prior authorization

Disclosure authorization forms are required by law to be prescribed and approved by the state insurance commissioner. The disclosure form must be written in accordance with the plain language laws of the state, and dated. Disclosure forms state the types of persons authorized to disclose private and personal information (e.g., neighbors, employers, and previous or other insurers); the kind of information which may be disclosed (e.g., personal habits, work habits, health habits such as smoking and drinking). The form must also state the reason information is collected, and how it will be used. For instance, the reason personal information is gathered is because the applicant requested a life insurance policy; the information will be used by the underwriting department for the purpose of determining the applicant's risk category.

The applicant's signature on the disclosure form authorizes the insurer to collect and disseminate information in the manner described in the notice. The authorization is only good for a certain period of time. For example, if authorization is given to an insurer to collect information with regard to a claim settlement, the authorization is good for 30 months. At the end of this period another authorization must be obtained. The applicant or insured may request, and receive, a copy of the authorization form.

Personal information may be disclosed to persons other than the requesting parties under certain conditions. Among those to whom an insurer may disclose information are agents, other insurers, insurance organizations (such as the Medical Information Bureau) and state insurance departments. This type of third-party disclosure may require authorization, but in some instances authorization is not required, as long as the applicant or insured has received proper notification of the insurer's information practices. In some cases information is passed on to those conducting scientific research, audits, or marketing approaches.

Underwriting

Consumers have the right to be treated fairly by an insurer's underwriting guidelines. This means that the guidelines used for underwriting a company's insurance policies should have a sound actuarial basis, be relevant to the risks being insured, and be applied uniformly to people of the same class.

Because underwriting is one of the key elements reviewed during a market conduct examination, it is important that the home office files be well documented with regard to underwriting guidelines, actions, and decisions. Market conduct examiners randomly sample company records to be sure that underwriting decisions are not unfairly discriminatory and are sufficiently documented. Examiners will also look for company memos and other internal communications that evidence anti-competitive behavior. However, the most commonly uncovered underwriting violations involve errors in the underwriting process (failure to follow established underwriting guidelines) rather than instances of unfair underwriting practices.

Redlining

The term **redlining** originated from the actual drawing of red lines around geographic areas considered by insurers too risky to write insurance business. The NAIC's Unfair Trade Practices Act was amended in the 1970s to prohibit unfair discrimination based on the geographic location and age of a residential property (however, actuarially sound discrimination is permissible). Redlining is now considered to include other types of unfair discrimination such as that based on marital status, age of home, or prior terminations of coverage or rejections. Allegations of redlining come up most often in urban, poor, minority, and/or rural risks.

There is mounting public concern for available and affordable insurance products in urban areas. The perception is that urban insurance rates do not encourage fair market competition, and that some insurers engage in unfairly discriminatory sales, marketing, underwriting, and distribution practices in order to avoid writing insurance business in undesirable areas. Studies show that urban residents have limited access to limited coverages from a limited number of companies, for which they pay higher-than-

Insurance as a Social Issue

It may be that actuarial issues are being confused with social issues. As for-profit entities, it may not be up to the insurance companies to ensure that every risk can buy insurance.

Insurance companies emphasize they have the right to be discriminatory; they just can't be *unfairly* discriminatory.

Some risks are located in areas that present an increased risk of loss, and insurance companies maintain they must be able to either decline to issue coverage or charge a correspondingly higher premium.

standard premiums and are subject to more frequent policy cancellations and nonrenewals.

In September 1995, Illinois Insurance Director Mark Boozell, responded to charges of redlining in Chicago by stating that evidence of "systematic discrimination against urban homeowners has not surfaced through market conduct exams, zip code data, or an unusual number of complaints either in the aggregate or against any one company."

Regulators traditionally review and approve insurance rates, but are otherwise unable to address availability and affordability issues. But some regulators and consumer organizations believe redlining persists. A 1995 Missouri study found that the underwriting guidelines of 14 insurers offering homeowners insurance violated the state's Unfair Trade Practices law. Similarly, a 1995 survey of underwriting practices conducted by the New Jersey Insurance Department, which was prompted by consumer complaints, found some insurers lacked written underwriting guidelines altogether, and those being used by other insurers were too vague to be consistently and uniformly applied.

Changes to Georgia's residential property underwriting regulations proposed early in 1996 would prohibit underwriting criteria based on:

- ✔ Marital status of the applicant, insured, or other person residing in the household
- ✔ Length of time at the address
- ✔ Employment status (including length of time employed)
- ✔ Level of education of the applicant or insured
- ✔ Failure of applicant or insured to purchase an additional policy which he or she did not request
- ✔ Age of dwelling (without considering updated systems)
- ✔ Applicant's status as a member of the armed forces

Such groupings would be considered unfairly discriminatory by the regulations if they are not actuarially supported, not relevant to the risk, or are based directly or indirectly on race or ethnicity.

Insurers claim that their own efforts to promote urban

insurance availability and discontinue unfair underwriting practices have effectively eliminated redlining. The Independent Insurance Agents of America (IIAA) has been particularly proactive in initiating programs to combat redlining, by working with minority and inner-city students, and by creating the Urban Opportunities & Minority Agents Task Force.

The NAIC's Insurance Availability and Affordability Task Force continues to examine the issues involved by conducting studies on insurance availability and cost in urban areas, and evaluate regulatory or policy measures that may be used to address these problems.

New Issues in Unfair Discrimination

Credit Reports. A debate has arisen over the insurance industry's use of credit reports as a factor in underwriting. It is questionable whether an individual's financial and credit history are relevant to whether the individual poses a higher or lower degree of insurance risk. Studies have shown a correlation between credit history and insurance loss, but whether credit history can legitimately be used in underwriting is debatable. An automobile insurer that uses credit cardholder status as underwriting criteria for private passenger underwriting contends that cardholders are better risks (have more favorable claims experience). But industry critics have questioned whether this is an invisible redlining technique. Having a credit card may just make an applicant more likely to be able to pay his or her insurance premiums.

An NAIC Subgroup is investigating the use of credit reports in underwriting and its implications under the Unfair Trade Practices Act. Initial findings indicate the reports are used with little consistency or accuracy in their application or interpretation. An NAIC "white paper" questions whether credit reports are being used in place of specifically prohibited discriminatory practices and the result is a "disproportionate impact" on certain (racial) groups. Insurers who use credit reports in underwriting should have "objective, documented, and measurable standards for their use." Unfortunately, the largest supplier of credit information, Fair, Isaac & Co, considers the information proprietary, so any correlation is difficult to establish.

Florida has proposed regulations that require insurers to notify applicants when their credit histories are being used in underwriting and requires carriers to keep records for five years so the DOI could review declinations as well as approvals. The proposed regulations have been put on hold due to challenges from insurance industry trade groups and carriers.

HIV/AIDS. Acquired immune deficiency syndrome (AIDS) has had a large impact on the insurance industry. The cost of AIDS to employers and insurers in the 1990s will be in the tens of billions. The costs associated with AIDS (prolonged medical care, expensive drug treatments, premature death) affect medical, disability, and life insurance coverages.

Failing to Observe Deadlines

A March, 1996 New York market conduct investigation of Motors Insurance Corporation uncovered that the company had failed to resolve auto insurance claims within specified time frames and failed to provide insureds with notices explaining the delays in claims payments.

The company also undervalued stolen or "totaled" vehicles and did not report losses to the National Insurance Crime Bureau as required within specified time limits.

The company was fined $16,200 and compelled to remit underpayments to claimants.

Blood testing for AIDS prior to policy issuance has become a common underwriting practice, especially when large amounts of life insurance are being requested. The proposed insured must acknowledge and consent to the blood test. Each insurance company sets its own guidelines for the ages and amounts of insurance that will require both a physical exam and blood test.

Most states have adopted legislation prohibiting unfair discrimination in underwriting criteria for AIDS testing. For example, in California, when deciding whether to test for HIV antibodies, insurers may not consider:

- Sexual orientation
- Marital status
- Living arrangements
- Occupation
- Gender
- Beneficiary designation
- Zip codes or other territorial classifications

Insurers knowingly violating these requirements can be fined up to $5,000.

Many states have also adopted specific guidelines for informing life insurance applicants who test positive for HIV antibodies, and for ensuring the confidentiality of their results.

Domestic Abuse. Allegations of unfair discrimination against applicants for health insurance have arisen after studies have shown that "domestic abuse status" is considered in underwriting applicants for accident and health insurance. A Washington state study showed 26% of carriers writing more than 70% of the accident and health insurance premium volume consider domestic abuse as an underwriting criteria. Model legislation has been proposed in a few states to limit or restrict such underwriting practices. Pennsylvania passed legislation in April 1996 prohibiting insurance companies from denying, cancelling, or refusing to renew insurance policies, or restricting coverage, adding surcharges, excluding benefits, or applying an adverse rating factor to a victim of domestic violence. The legislation addresses all lines of insurance, and includes strict confidentiality requirements.

Post Claims Underwriting

Post claims underwriting is an illegal practice where the insurance company voids or attempts to void a life, or more commonly, a health insurance policy after a claim has been submitted.

Life and health policies are issued based upon the applicant's responses to questions on the application designed to determine the applicant's health status. The time to conduct comprehensive underwriting and clear up any questions is before a claim arises, not after.

For example, if an applicant lists prescribed medications (such as insulin) which are commonly used to treat a medical condition (such as diabetes) for which coverage would otherwise be denied, and the policy is issued anyway, the policy may not be later rescinded when a claim arises related to that condition. The policy can only be rescinded or benefits denied if the applicant's responses on the application were incorrect or untrue.

Disclosure of Underwriting Guidelines

In questioning how the information available to consumers affects the availability and affordability of insurance, the NAIC is examining the controversial subject of public access to insurers underwriting guidelines.

Insurers view their underwriting practices as proprietary information, even trade secrets, and say allowing public access would be a disincentive to product innovation, would reduce competition in the marketplace, reduce availability of insurance products, and would encourage fraud.

Consumer advocates claim public access would promote competitiveness, availability, and innovation, and would promote loss prevention and encourage the use of risk-related guidelines. Most states require the filing of written underwriting guidelines, but the filed guidelines are kept confidential. Florida considers filed underwriting guidelines public information. And newly proposed legislation in Georgia requires the disclosure of company underwriting guidelines to agents (but not the public).

Denying Rightful Claims Without Grounds

"We had a credit life and accident company using unlicensed persons to sell insurance, having licensed producers illegally pre-sign insurance applications, using claim forms that did not match the coverage in the policies at issue, and then denying rightful claims without grounds," reports Gene Reed, licensing director at the Delaware Insurance Department. Even after the DOI informed them a claim was justified and should be paid, the company's compliance analyst responded that the Delaware regulators were misreading their own regulations and denied coverage.

The result: the company was ordered to pay the claim immediately, was fined $15,000, and required to prove they are taking steps to come into compliance with Delaware regulations. The insurance agency was also fined $5,000. "They could have saved themselves a lot of trouble if they had just paid a straightforward $9,000 claim in the first place," says Reed.

Claims Settlement Practices

The claims settlement practices of insurers are regulated, in the public interest, for two main reasons:

- ✔ Insurance companys collect policyowner's money for the purpose of settling claims
- ✔ When insureds' claims are denied, or claim payments are delayed or altered, the consequences go beyond the policy benefits, and can drastically affect other areas of the insured's financial situation

One way for an insurer to lead by example is by rigorous compliance with Unfair Claims Practices laws. The public expects quick and fair settlement of its claims. It is the insurer's responsibility to establish necessary claims processing procedures which will enable all claims to be settled promptly and fairly. Typically, agents do not become directly involved in the claims process (unless delays and problems arise); the insurer's claims personnel do. It is thus important that claims personnel be trained properly and understand the needs of the claimants.

Penalties

Following an investigation and a hearing, if the state insurance department finds that an insurance company has engaged in any unfair trade or unfair claims practice, the commissioner may issue a cease and desist order prohibiting the individual or company from continuing the practice. Failure to comply with a cease and desist order can result in a substantial fine (usually $10,000, but these amounts differ by state). In addition, fines and loss of license may also be imposed for any company or person guilty of violating the Unfair Trade Practices Act.

Unfair Claims Settlement Laws

The Unfair Claims Settlement Practices provisions of the Unfair Trade Practices Act (a model NAIC Act which has been adopted in all states) are designed to protect the insureds and claimants from any claims settlement practices which are unfair, deceptive or misleading.

The following are considered unfair claims practices:

- ✔ Misrepresenting pertinent facts or insurance policy provisions relating to coverage at issue

More Improper Claims Denials

In August 1996, Oregon leveled a $15,000 civil penalty against Qual-Med of Oregon for improper claims denials. A routine market conduct examination revealed a pattern of denying payment for emergency room claims without first conducting a reasonable investigation to determine the validity of the claims, as required by law.

"In three cases cited in our order, Qual-Med denied emergency room claims only to find out later that the claimants had been referred to the emergency room by a doctor with responsibility for making such referrals under Qual-Med's health plan," said Oregon Insurance Commissioner Kerry Barnett.

Qual-Med was also cited for recordkeeping violations that made it impossible for investigators to determine whether policyholders had received fair treatment at claims time.

This action, along with a $20,000 penalty imposed against PacifiCare earlier this year for improper emergency room claims denials and inadequate recordkeeping, reflects a new focus on closer scrutiny of the market practices of health insurance companies in Oregon.

- ✔ Failure to acknowledge and act reasonably promptly upon communications with respect to claims arising under insurance policies
- ✔ Failing to adopt and implement reasonable standards for the prompt investigation of claims arising under insurance policies
- ✔ Refusing to pay claims without conducting a reasonable investigation based upon all available information
- ✔ Failing to affirm or deny coverage of claims within a reasonable time after proof of loss statements have been completed
- ✔ Not attempting in good faith to effectuate prompt, fair, and equitable settlements of claims in which liability has become reasonably clear
- ✔ Compelling insureds to institute litigation to recover amounts due under an insurance policy by offering substantially less than the amounts ultimately recovered in actions brought by such insureds
- ✔ Attempting to settle a claim for less than the amount to which a reasonable person would have believed he or she was entitled by reference to written or principal advertising material accompanying or made part of an application
- ✔ Attempting to settle claims on the basis of an application which was altered without notice, knowledge or consent of the insured
- ✔ Making claims payments to insureds or beneficiaries not accompanied by statements setting forth the coverage under which the payments are being made
- ✔ Making known to insureds or claimants a policy of appealing from arbitration awards in favor of insureds or claimants for the purpose of compelling them to accept settlements or compromises less than the amount awarded in arbitration
- ✔ Delaying the investigation or payment of a claim by requiring an insured, claimant, or the physician of either, to submit a preliminary claim report and then requiring the subsequent submission of formal proof of loss forms, both of which submissions contain substantially the same information

Error Ratios as High as 88%

A 1996 news release reporting the results of one market conduct exam in Pennsylvania revealed that agents routinely "concealed replacement activity on applications ... for the purpose of increasing their commissions and inflating sales reports."

The same investigation found that the company was deficient in fulfilling state replacement requirements: its files had error ratios that were as high as 88%.

The company was fined for failing to have "essential internal controls which would have detected such problems."

- ✔ Failing to promptly settle claims where liability has become reasonably clear under one portion of the insurance policy coverage in order to influence settlement under other portions of the insurance policy coverage
- ✔ Failing to promptly provide a reasonable explanation of the basis relied on in the insurance policy in relation to the facts or applicable law for denial of a claim or for the offer of a compromise settlement

Some states have added another provision which makes it an unfair claim practice to offer a settlement or payment in any manner prohibited by law.

Cancellations/Nonrenewals

Policyholders have the right to expect fair treatment from insurers when it comes to policy cancellations and nonrenewals. State insurance statutes define the amount of advance notice required before certain types of policies may be cancelled/nonrenewed, and some even restrict policy cancellations by limiting the reasons upon which the insurance company may base its decision to terminate a policy.

Market conduct examiners determine compliance by examining random samples of an insurer's cancelled policies by line of insurance. The examiners also check to make sure return premiums on cancelled policies have been calculated accurately. If inaccuracies are discovered, the examiners will require that refunds be made.

Common Violations of Cancellation/Nonrenewal Practices

Summaries of state disciplinary actions against insurers are saturated with company violations of the rules regarding policy cancellations and nonrenewals. Some examples:

- ✔ Failing to follow state guidelines for policy cancellation
- ✔ Failing to observe cancellation/nonrenewal requirements as stated in the policy
- ✔ Failing to send nonrenewal notices in a timely manner
- ✔ Failing to specify the reasons for nonrenewal on nonrenewal notices sent to insureds
- ✔ Failing to provide insureds with their history of insurance losses with nonrenewal notices (where required)

Policy Replacement

The duties of agents and insurers during the replacement of a life or health insurance policy were discussed at length in Chapter 2. Clearly, the insurance company owes it to its policyholders to comply with the minimum standards imposed by state law with regard to policy replacements.

However, recent market conduct exam results indicate that insurers should also have in place reporting systems which track the number of policy replacements (especially internally replaced policies), to help identify where improper policy replacements may be occurring.

Communication of company replacement guidelines from management down to the agency force is important, as are responsible and consistent disciplinary practices. The multistate investigation of Prudential uncovered weak and ineffective communication between management and agents. Conflicts between company policy and state replacement regulations, as well as failure to responsibly and consistently discipline its agents, compounded Prudential's problems. In fact, the executive summary report noted that "even when there were multiple instances of undisclosed replacements, the company seldom took any disciplinary action."

WANTED: Any Warm, Live Body

Jim Genetti, supervisor of licensing and continuing education for the Idaho Insurance Department, stresses "It is important for companies to pay attention to the quality of the people they license. Some companies will appoint any warm live body, even one with a 10-page rap sheet."

Specialty Lines: Home Service

Home service insurance is any insurance product which is marketed, sold, delivered, issued, and serviced, and where premiums are collected on a monthly or more frequent basis at the policyholder's home or business. Home service insurance is distinguished from "industrial" life insurance, which is usually statutorily defined by state law as having a face amount of less than $2,000, premiums based on the Commissioners Standard Industrial tables and premiums payable monthly. However, in many states the terms debit, home service, monthly debit, etc. are interchangeable with regard to this type of insurance.

As the sales and marketing practices of the whole life insurance industry have come under increasing scrutiny, special attention is being paid to the home services industry. A special working group of the NAIC Market Conduct and Consumer Affairs Subcommittee has been formed to study and make recommendations regarding the marketing and sales practices of home services companies. The working group's concern is that insurance (both life/health and property/casualty) being delivered via the home service method of marketing appears to be "inferior to that of other

Advice to Companies: Get the Certification

"We have approximately 2,250 companies and 80,000 agents in Virginia," says Warren Spruill, supervisor of agent's licensing. "I'd like to think 79,995 are good agents, but there's always a few bad ones out there.

"The best document for the hiring of a new agent is the certification from the applicant's home state insurance department. It will denote the agent's name, address, method of qualification, lines of authority (license types), date of issue, compliance with continuing education, and will reflect any administrative or disciplinary actions."

Don't just ask for a copy of the agent's license and have that be enough for an appointment, advises Spruill. It could be a copy of an old license. For example, the agent could have had that license revoked for failure to forward premiums, and may actually hold a newer license, but the company will never know about the prior revocation.

insurers" and that premiums are excessive or otherwise inequitable.

For example, a survey conducted in four states of companies offering property insurance through home service indicates that dwelling and homeowner policies routinely do not include liability coverage or replacement cost coverage, and the premiums charged are higher for lesser amounts of coverage than those charged by other "standard" insurers. (In fact, in states where a FAIR plan operates, the home service insurers were found to charge more for coverage than the FAIR plan.) Concerns have also been expressed over whether agent commission rates in this industry are excessive.

Home service insurers reported using agents who hold temporary licenses to market new policies (perhaps not the best business practice) and experience high agent turnover (up to 50% annually). Obviously problems can arise whenever agents are collecting premiums paid in cash, but other improprieties can surface in the improper recording of agent collections, agents overcharging for policy premiums, or not submitting collections as required.

Suggestions for improving the home service area include requiring fidelity bonds of agents accepting premiums, better controls on policy numbering, policy receipts, and internal audits.

Due Diligence in Hiring Agents

Studies by LIMRA International show that while the public's view of life insurance agents in general is poor (somewhere below lawyers and used car salespersons), in general the public holds their own personal agent in high regard. (Similar studies by the IIAA reflect similar public attitudes towards property/casualty agents.)

The truth is, there are plenty of good agents out there, providing excellent advice and service, clearly explaining the policies they sell, and fairly representing their insurance companies. It's the poorly trained, dishonest, self-serving agents that give the business a bad name.

Insurance companies can be held partly to blame for these problems. Insurance agents are recruited from a wide range of sources, sent through selection and screening processes of questionable usefulness, trained, licensed, and rushed into the field where immediate sales are demanded. The result is often a staggering turnover. In the life insurance industry, four year agent retention is estimated at just 20-25%.

Insurance companies owe it to their policyholders to recruit and hire competent insurance agents to represent their products to consumers. Stringent selection standards are in order, particularly in conducting background checks and following up on employment histories and references. Many companies are developing "due diligence" committees that oversee the agent recruiting process.

Unfortunately, it appears that companies take an equally big risk when they hire new, inexperienced agents as they do when they hire experienced agents who may be company jumping. Recruits who are properly investigated, properly trained, properly motivated, and provided with adequate support systems can succeed. To bring in recruits any other way is just asking for trouble.

State Requirements for Background Investigations

State guidelines for appointing new agents vary, but basically all require the company to certify the prospective appointee's "trustworthiness, suitability, and competency" prior to appointment.

Some states also require companies to certify that an investigation has been completed as to the character and ability of the applicant and certify that the company is satisfied that the applicant is "of good moral character, financially responsible, and trustworthy." Others go so far as conducting their own criminal and/or credit background investigations of new or newly appointed agents.

Because state guidelines for conducting background investigations tend to be vague, they have proven especially confusing to those companies appointing agents in all 50 states. What exactly constitutes a reasonable inquiry into an individual's background? And to what extent (and expense) is a company expected to go in order to be satisfied as to an applicant's qualifications?

Aetna looks at the individual's credit background, criminal convictions, department of insurance background, and bankruptcies, depending on their age and circumstances, reports Richard Heffernon, compliance superintendent.

Advice to Companies: Wait for the Results

Although background investigations are time consuming, one thing is clear: companies should wait until the results are in before appointing the agent.

"If you're foolish enough to appoint someone before the conclusion of the background investigation, then you're just asking for trouble," warns Richard Heffernon, compliance superintendent for Aetna Life Insurance/Aetna Health Plans.

Foolishness aside, a company who appoints an agent before the background investigation is completed is most likely in violation of state law.

Prostitution Not Related to Insurance Business

"We received an insurance license application from a person who had a prostitution conviction within the past five years," reports one regulator. "We received a letter from the applicant explaining the circumstances of the conviction, and since the conviction had nothing to do with the insurance business, we granted the license and the person is now gainfully employed."

Northland evaluates agents on a case-by-case basis. If they've been convicted of a felony involving breach of trust and/or dishonesty "an appointment is highly unlikely", according to Christine Williams, licensing administrator.

"We want to comply but we can't get our hands around what exactly is required by each state," complains Linda Harrell, a licensing consultant for CNA. "Is it a credit check? A criminal background investigation? Do we also need to check education and experience? Employment history? References?"

State regulators and legal compliance staff are reluctant to be more specific. For example, if the regulators were to say that conducting a criminal and credit background check is sufficient, and a problem arises, they wouldn't want to be limited by their own definitions. Regulators make it clear the ultimate responsibility rests with the appointing company even when a background check isn't required by law.

A further wrinkle to agent appointments and background investigations is the Federal Crime Bill of 1994, which imposes criminal penalties on anyone who allows a person convicted of a felony, or an act involving dishonesty or breach of trust, to participate in the insurance industry. A national search for background information such as this could cost thousands of dollars per applicant. This provision of the law is still being clarified, and it remains unclear how the U.S. Justice Department will enforce this law.

Criminal and/or Credit Background?

Just conducting a criminal background check may not be enough. Some insurers report they see a correlation between an applicant's credit history and future agent behavior. Other companies consider poor credit histories as just part of the total picture when deciding to contract with a producer.

Many states ask license applicants to disclose bankruptcies, but acknowledge the difficulty of using bankruptcy as an indication of financial standing. Is the bankruptcy cleared? Was it personal or business-related? How long ago did it happen? For the most part, personal bankruptcies and tax liens are overlooked unless they have to do with misappropriation of funds. In Tennessee, agents are asked to disclose any bankruptcies on their license renewal form, and must file copies of the bankruptcy documents. However, the DOI inquires further only if the bankruptcy had to do with the insurance business.

Examples of Different State Approaches

Pennsylvania requires the appointing company to verify employment history, references, current address, and make "reasonable inquiry" into the person's background. The company background check is expected to be independent of the check performed by the insurance department. Pennsylvania then conducts its own criminal background check (this requirement went into effect after the Pennsylvania Commissioner learned an agent had been appointed while serving time in federal prison).

Any applicant who has a felony conviction within the past five years is automatically denied, as well as anyone who has misappropriated funds regardless of how long ago. If an agent's license is revoked "back to day 1" and the DOI learns the company never performed the required background check, the company could be held responsible for the policies sold by and commissions paid to that agent, warns Peter Salvatore, director of producer licensing.

Kentucky requires companies to inquire into the agent's qualifications, reputation, and criminal history. Texas is considering requiring criminal background checks in addition to credit checks as part of the appointment process (applicants with histories of bankruptcy are subject to further DOI review), but the state clearly holds the company "responsible for all agent acts."

Idaho requires the appointing company to verify the applicant's "trustworthiness" and conduct a background check. Idaho also conducts a routine FBI background investigation of its own on all new applicants.

West Virginia requires a background investigation for each resident and nonresident appointment, even if the agent is already appointed with other companies.

"It's important for a copy of the background investigation report to be in company files," advises Jane Strother, director of agent licensing and education for West Virginia. "We may never ask for it, but if we are investigating a consumer complaint and it's not there, someone in my department is going to be very upset with the company."

Delaware requires that the company investigate the agent's background to be sure the applicant is "competent, trustworthy, financially responsible and of good reputation." (Crimi-

Advice to Companies: Appoint Agents Before They Write Business

In Illinois there is a $50 penalty per application received from an unlicensed producer; this goes up to $100 per application if the violation is a repeat violation.

In Colorado, accepting business from an agent who is not yet appointed results in a $500 fine.

In Missouri, receiving applications from an unlicensed agent results in a $100 fine per occurrence. Paying commissions to an unlicensed agent is also $100 per occurrence. Failing to notify the DOI of an agent appointment is $25 per occurrence.

nal investigations are not required by statute.) Delaware considers the nature of credit problems and will not deny agent licenses based on personal bankruptcy. The DOI wants to see the background investigation with the initial application, but if the individual has been with the company for more than one year the company can just certify the person has been checked out.

"It happens that we'll run a retail credit check and find massive debt and bankruptcies on people who were 'certified' by the company," reports Gene Reed, director of licensing. "If there's a consumer complaint, we'll go right to the agency records and see how the money's being handled."

In Tennessee, the individual applying for a license does not need a company sponsor, so there is no requirement for a background investigation at that time, according to T.A. Patterson, director of the agent licensing division at the Tennessee Department of Insurance. The answers to the questions on the application regarding past convictions, felony misdemeanors, and bankruptcy are the responsibility of the individual applying for the license.

At the time of appointment, the company must declare it has checked the background of the agent and the agent has shown himself competent and trustworthy. "We would assume the companies know the insurance laws with regard to the statutory reasons for license denial, suspension, and revocation, and that the company would cover all of those areas in the background investigation," says Patterson.

"We do find we've received falsified applications and that can result in license denial or revocation," says Patterson. "Company compliance directives often ask agents to report suspected misconduct on the part of other agents. And agents do report each other. So eventually we find out about their convictions and felony misdemeanors."

In Rhode Island, the state conducts a criminal background check on all resident agents through the attorney general's office which shows the date and disposition of any Rhode Island arrests. Applications are denied on a case-by-case basis, explains Robert Powers, legal counsel to the Rhode Island DOI.

Hiring Outside Firms to Conduct Background Investigations

Many insurance companies hire outside firms to conduct detailed background investigations, learn about criminal records, bankruptcies, or, if the person is also licensed as a broker/dealer or registered respresentative, problems with the Central Registration Depository maintained by the National Association of Securities Dealers (NASD).

Some in the industry complain that such detailed investigations are expensive and time consuming. Searches can cost upwards of $30 and take from

3 days to 3 weeks to complete. Sometimes the insurance company absorbs the cost of the background check, or the agent may be assessed the cost until his or her premium volume reaches a certain amount, at which time he or she will be reimbursed.

"Insurance carriers realize that many market conduct issues relate directly to the producer selection process," says Stefan Keller, vice president of the Business Information Group, a Philadelphia firm that provides insurers with pre-contractual and pre-appointment background investigations on insurance agents.

"Information obtained from background investigations has a direct impact on market conduct. Without the necessary background information, companies have very little protection from the rogue agents, or bad apples," advises Keller. "Carriers use the information to help ensure a high-quality distribution force. This not only helps protect companies from regulatory, legal, and other market conduct problems, it helps keep unscrupulous agents out of the business and away from the public."

By conducting background investigations, and gathering information about the potential agent's financial history (including bankruptcies), criminal history, civil litigation history, education history, military record, employment or contracting history, insurance licensing history, and securities licensing history, carriers are better able to make informed decisions about appointing their agents. Keller reports that most agents support the use of background investigations because they help ensure that good agents won't have to compete with unethical or underhanded competition.

Producer Licensing and Appointment

The producer licensing and appointment portion of a market conduct exam looks at how well a company is complying with state licensing laws and regulations. Examiners will compare the department of insurance listing of licensed/appointed producers with the company's listing, and the department's list of terminated producers with the company's listing. Discrepancies are almost certain to be rigorously investigated.

In most states, you cannot produce (write business) until you are appointed as an agent with an insurance company. Patsy Papandrea Jr., former director of agent licensing in Connecticut (now a regulatory consultant), notes that in a market conduct review, the department will instantly note if an agent was not appointed at the time of sale.

Dennis Poppenhagen, former director of licensing in Minnesota, agrees. "Be very careful with this issue," he warns. "The agent will be sanctioned and the company fined."

Procedures for appointing producers, copies of producer licenses, notices of appointment, producer contracts, lines of authority, lists of commissions paid, and procedures for producer termination will also be reviewed. Producer termination records may be inspected to be sure the reasons for termination are documented, and where termination is for cause, that the department of insurance has been notified.

Companies must keep accurate copies of agent licenses and other required forms, and keep painstakingly accurate reconciliation records. Red flags go up whenever company records differ from those of the department of insurance.

The most common violations discovered during this part of a routine market conduct examination (and the most common reasons for companies receiving fines and penalties) include:

- ✔ Paying commissions to unlicensed agents
- ✔ Accepting applications from unlicensed or non-appointed agents
- ✔ Failure to notify the insurance department of appointment and termination of agents
- ✔ Paying commissions without having a copy of the agent/agency's license on file
- ✔ Failure to maintain agent licensing records

(Of course, there are technical state-to-state differences. In Louisiana, an agent can write business before being appointed, but cannot receive commission until after the appointment goes into effect.)

The following pages will review the common state requirements for agent licensing, education, examinations, appointment, renewal, and termination, which insurance companies are expected to monitor.

License Required

Under the statutes of most states, no person is permitted to be, or act as, an insurance agent, broker, or solicitor unless currently licensed as such. In many states, adjusters, consultants, and service representatives must also be licensed.

No agent, broker, or solicitor may receive applications for, process or place any kinds of insurance for which he or she is not currently licensed. Also, in most states, agents are prohibited from placing insurance with any insurer with which the agent does not then hold both a license and appointment as agent.

State licensing regulations commonly identify:

- ✔ Who is eligible to become an insurance agent (for example, those with good moral character, or who are 18 years or older)
- ✔ Who is ineligible to become an insurance agent (such as, those found guilty of dishonesty, or those convicted of a felony)
- ✔ How to apply for an agent license
- ✔ Who must take and pass a qualifying examination (for example, agents, brokers, and solicitors)
- ✔ Who is exempt from the examination (such as those holding designations, or limited lines agents such as ticket-selling agents of airlines)
- ✔ Types of licenses required (agent, broker, temporary)
- ✔ Educational requirements (prelicensing education needed prior to taking the exam and/or continuing education requirements)
- ✔ How to maintain an insurance license (expiration and renewal of license)
- ✔ Conditions for suspension, revocation, or nonrenewal of the license

Qualifications — Agents, Brokers, Solicitors

To be eligible for a license as an agent, broker or solicitor, an individual typically must meet the following requirements:

- ✔ Be at least 18 years of age
- ✔ Depending on the state, be a citizen of the United States, or have applied with the U.S. Department of Immigration for permanent residence and have declared the intent to apply for citizenship
- ✔ Have been a bona fide resident of the state in which application is being made for whatever amount of time the state requires
- ✔ Be trustworthy, have a good reputation, and not have been convicted of a felony or a crime involving moral turpitude
- ✔ If applying for a brokers license, have filed any bond which may be required and be able to demonstrate to the satisfaction of the insurance department that the necessary competency exists due to experience or special education to fulfill a broker's responsibilities
- ✔ Have complied with any required prelicensing education laws and pass the required licensing examination in order to demonstrate competency in the kinds of insurance to be transacted under the license

When Agents Fail to Complete Continuing Education

Delaware recently suspended 301 resident and 1836 nonresident licenses for failure to comply with continuing education requirements. So far, the department has reinstated 300 of these agents and collected $20,600 in fines.

An agent who had his insurance license revoked in Kansas for failing to provide evidence of continuing education compliance was then fined $500 by the New York DOI for failing to disclose the revocation on his New York license renewal application.

- ✔ Intend to actively engage in the insurance business with members of the public, and not use the license principally for transacting a disproportionate amount of controlled business

Application for License

Application for an insurance license is made to the state insurance department on whatever forms have been designated and furnished for that purpose. Licenses are issued upon proper filing of the application, satisfaction of all statutory requirements, and payment of the appropriate fee. Applications usually require personal information including the identity, personal history, business record, and insurance experience of the applicant, along with a statement about the purpose for which the license will be used. Applications frequently include the following questions:

- ✔ Whether or not the applicant was ever previously licensed to transact any kind of insurance in any state
- ✔ Whether or not any license was ever refused, suspended or revoked
- ✔ Whether or not the applicant is indebted to any insurer or general agent
- ✔ Whether or not the applicant has ever had an agency contract cancelled

If a firm or corporation applies for an agent or broker license, similar information is required with regard to the firm or corporation, as well as the names of all members, officers, and directors of the firm or corporation. Each person who is to exercise agent or broker powers must be identified and must furnish the same personal information required of an individual applicant.

Misrepresentations on License Applications

Incredibly, some of the biggest problems encountered by state regulators involve misrepresentations on the initial agent license application.

"You're hoping that they're answering the application questions truthfully," says West Virginia's Jane Strother. "It's a notarized signature, for whatever that's worth."

Joyce Bryant, assistant licensing director for Kentucky, reports that applicants routinely answer "no" or "not applicable" when asked whether they have ever held an insurance license, even if they have. The application is rejected and the individual is given a chance to reapply. Believe it or not, these individuals subsequently fail to indicate "yes" on the second application when asked if they've ever had an application rejected. Upon the second misrepresentation to the DOI, they are subject to fines.

When asked about their criminal history background, some applicants either don't read the question, or forget about a youthful public intoxication or shoplifting conviction, or are too embarrassed to write it down, hoping that it's "off the records", according to William Elkjer, deputy commissioner of agent licensing in Texas. "If they'd been honest in the first place they would've gone right through the process," he says. "Being truthful makes it go a lot smoother."

Even worse, the misrepresentations can multiply. Suppose an applicant denies a criminal conviction on a series of applications or renewals. "The regulators will think, 'This guy's been lying to us for years!' and it can result in a severe fine or denied license," says Elkjer. "We've denied 40 applications in the last four months for misrepresentations."

Licensing Examination

Unless otherwise exempted by state law, applicants for an insurance license must take and pass an examination testing the applicant's knowledge of both insurance and related legal responsibilities. Examinations may not be required for:

- ✔ Those applying for and meeting the requirements for temporary licenses
- ✔ Nonresident agent applicants who reside in a reciprocal state
- ✔ Transportation ticket agents of common carriers applying for a limited license to sell only travel accident insurance and baggage insurance
- ✔ Title insurance agents
- ✔ Applicants for a license covering the same kinds of insurance for which he or she was previously licensed in the same state within the previous 12 months

Common Violations

State files of administrative actions against agents commonly list "failure to report an administrative action taken by another state" as the reason for fines and other penalties.

Even though agents are supposed to report disciplinary actions, they often fail to do so.

Some actual cases: A Texas agent failed to inform the Texas Insurance Department of an action by another state and was fined $1,500. In Wisconsin, an agent guilty of the same violation was fined $250 and forced to surrender his license.

Regulatory Information Retrieval System

State insurance departments keep lists of agents with formal disciplinary records: license suspensions or revocations. However, the public record doesn't show pending actions or customer complaints. A national database of all actions taken against insurance agents and firms is maintained by the National Association of Insurance Commissioners (NAIC). This database, the Regulatory Information Retrieval System (RIRS) contains information on more than 60,000 agents and companies against whom disciplinary action has been taken (including suspensions, revocations, fines/penalties, cease and desist orders, consent orders, etc.) The information (which is publicly available) is updated monthly and is used by both companies and states for background checks on agents and potential agents.

NAIC Database Products, (816) 374-7194

Once the individual has met all the qualification, application, examination, and other legal requirements, a license is issued which states the name of the licensee, issue date and expiration, kind(s) of insurance covered, and any other conditions which apply.

Continuation/Expiration/Renewal of License

Insurance agent licenses generally continue in force until their expiration dates, unless the license is revoked, suspended or terminated at an earlier date. Each state has established its own procedures for continuation and renewal of licenses. Renewal fees are normally charged.

Almost every state has established continuing education requirements for licensees, which require the agent to earn a specific number of continuing education credits through approved self-study or classroom programs in order to qualify for license renewal. Failure to comply with continuing education requirements will result in the license not being renewed.

A growing number of states are requiring that agents complete courses in **ethics** as a part of their continuing education requirements. For example, recently passed legislation in Georgia requires each agent to annually complete three hours of continuing education in the subject area of ethics. Other states with ethics requirements include Kansas, Indiana, Nebraska, New Mexico, Oklahoma, Oregon, Texas and Virginia.

Appointment of Agents

Each insurer appointing an agent is typically required to file the appointment with the insurance department in writing and pay the specified appointment fee. The filing specifies the kinds of insurance to be transacted by the agent.

Subject to continuation of the appointment and payment of the periodic continuation fee, appointments generally remain in effect until the agent's license is revoked or terminated. Appointments not continued by the periodic filing and payment of fees expire. Late charges may be added to the fee if a filing of an appointment is late.

It should be noted that the agent's **license** is with the **state** and the agent's **appointment** is with an **insurer**. Depending on the state, loss of an appointment does not necessarily mean that an agent has lost his or her license. It simply means that the agent may no longer represent that particular company although he or she may still be licensed with the state.

Termination of Appointment

Subject to an agent's contractual rights, if any, an insurer may terminate any of its appointed agents at any time. The insurer is required to give prompt written notice of the termination to the insurance department (and, of course, to the agent), and must file a statement of facts related to the termination and reasons for it.

New York goes so far as to require "...if any aspect of the cause for terminating the appointment of an agent relates to the trustworthiness or competency of that licensee it is incumbent upon the insurer to provide that information to the department in the termination notice regardless of whether the termination was by mutual consent." Failure to do so subjects the insurer to disciplinary action.

Barbara Cheles, director of agent and broker licensing in New York, notes that whenever an agent is terminated for cause, the DOI will investigate even if the company is already performing its own investigation. "All termination notices are privileged information," says Cheles, to encourage companies to be as explicit as possible in for-cause termination notices.

Efforts to Share Information

Clearly, insurance companies have more discretion in appointing agents than the state regulators do in licensing them. If an applicant for an insurance license has met all of the qualifying criteria, the state has no choice but to issue the license. And once an agent license is issued, it can take six months or more of administrative process (hearings, etc.) at the state level in order to have the license revoked.

Agents are supposed to report any out of state disciplinary actions to the resident state insurance department. Similarly, agents are expected to report disciplinary actions to their appointing company(ies) at the time of the violation, or no later than at license renewal, but this rarely happens. Insurance companies have found themselves in the embarrassing position of giving sales awards to an agent whose license is being revoked for violations of insurance law.

Better System Needed

Glenn Pomeroy, North Dakota Insurance Commissioner, is convinced that the biggest problems come from a small segment of the agent population: the "rogue" agent who doesn't follow the rules and leaves in his or her wake damaged policyholders. "The insurance industry needs a better system for spotting the bad apples and getting them out of the business," says Pomeroy.

Where Do the Bad Guys Go?

"Right now when an agent is fired for cause, it is very difficult to know what the agent does next," explains John Mancini, market affairs manager for the NAIC. "He or she may obtain an appointment with another company or may change state residence and continue to commit the same offenses.

"It would be of great benefit, both to regulators and the consumers they are trying to protect, knowing what an agent's licensing and appointment history is, knowing what an agent's regulatory history is, by tracking agents from state to state and company to company. If companies could share this information with each other through the Producer Information Network it would be beneficial to all parties."

Likewise, when agents are terminated for cause, the insurance company is supposed to notify the department of insurance. In practice, companies may be reluctant to call attention to their internal disciplinary actions. An agent facing complaints at one company can just switch to another company when the heat gets turned up. And the new company probably won't be the wiser.

Even when formal disciplinary action is taken, an agent may just move to another state and become licensed there, usually by falsifying the license application questions, "Have you ever been licensed as an insurance agent?" and "Have you ever had an insurance license revoked or suspended?". "It's those 'hopscotch artists' that pop in, tear the business out, and then move on, that give everyone a bad name, and probably have gotten market conduct the high prominence that it has now achieved" observes ACLI's Al Dawson.

Insurers should make use of the data on agents that already exists; especially when appointing new agents. However, the data in the NAIC databases comes from state insurance departments (not all states actively participate), and can be incomplete in areas where sharing of information is prohibited. Regulators and industry often complain that in too many instances the reason for agent termination is either unavailable or listed as an unhelpful "other". For example, a 1995 press release from the Illinois Department of Insurance announced the revocation of an insurance producer's license. During the DOI investigation, the producer requested voluntary revocation of his license, and because the department's investigatory files are deemed confidential, the reasons for the revocation cannot be made public.

The NAIC is also developing a producer information network (PIN) which will link all 50 states electronically (it is estimated that not all states will be supplying information until at least 1999).

As part of the PIN, the NAIC's producer database (PDB) will help states track individual agents from state to state, and will include both current and historical information on the producer. Through the PDB, disciplinary actions taken in one state can be automatically communicated to other states where the agent or firm may be operating. The database was made accessible to all states in June 1996, although only a few states are currently supplying data.

Features of the PDB include:

- ✔ Current and historical producer licensing information
- ✔ Tracking of agent certifications and letters of clearance
- ✔ NASD exams and disciplinary information
- ✔ Automatic notification to states of regulatory actions taken in other states
- ✔ Automatic notification to states when a producer's resident license is terminated

The PDB is linked to the Regulatory Information Retrieval System (RIRS). However, only final regulatory actions (and not pending actions) will be accessible through this link.

Pomeroy's prior experience as the North Dakota Securities Commissioner has led him to support the NAIC's PIN/PDB projects. Considering that SEC/NASD registration involves one application and one license, not 50 different applications and licenses, Pomeroy notes these NAIC projects will help bring in a system that makes sense to the industry.

Gene Reed, licensing director for the state of Delaware, sees the producer database as the solution to the problem of sharing information among states, and to the problem of bad agents. While Delaware files all its disciplinary actions with RIRS, the RIRS report alone is not accepted as a "background check".

It is also hoped that any movement towards multi-state market conduct examinations will help encourage some uniform agent licensing practices, something that has so far defied attempts at standardization.

Complaint Handling

Part of any routine market conduct exam is a review of complaint handling procedures. This includes both consumer grievances submitted in writing directly to the company as well as those filed with the department of insurance. Examiners usually select a random sample of complaints from the company's complaint register, and look for patterns of misconduct as well as frequency of specific types of complaints, which can uncover a larger problem within the company.

Six Complaint Trigger

In the New York Life class action lawsuit, it was disclosed that the insurance company used a "six-complaint trigger".

If the company had received six or more complaints against a particular agent it was considered a presumption of some wrongdoing by the agent requiring further investigation.

> **Optimistic Outlook**
>
> Some of the more proactive companies that have responded to the market conduct challenge by creating rigorous internal audit programs have a surprisingly optimistic outlook.
>
> "We're scheduled for two market conduct exams in two states for 1996," reports Wanda Smith, insurance chief compliance officer and government relations at Primerica Life Insurance Company.
>
> "It might sound crazy, but I'm actually looking forward to it. I think companies stand to benefit from the experience of market conduct examinations."

Examiners evaluate how promptly the company generally responds to consumer complaints, and review supporting documentation (claim files, company correspondence, underwriting files, etc.) to determine whether adequate steps have been taken in each case to resolve the problems. Examiners consider how the company uses the data from policyholder grievances as a management tool to improve company operations. Companies also are assigned a "complaint index" which may reveal areas in company operations that need correction.

In most states companies are required to maintain a complaint register that records all complaints as well as the insurer's response and final disposition of the complaints. Each insurer should have complaint handling procedures that have been clearly communicated to policyholders and to agents. Policyholders should be provided with a telephone number and address for complaints and inquiries regarding their coverage.

Some states compile and release annual consumer complaint ratios by insurance company (the Illinois Department of Insurance now includes this information on its web site). These should be considered only one part of the total picture for an insurer and are not intended for marketing purposes (i.e., it would be inappropriate to claim "We have a better complaint ratio than XYZ Company"). Complaint ratios released by the Illinois Insurance Department in July 1995 indicated 70% of the grievances against insurers involved claims handling, 13% underwriting, 10% policyholder service, and 7% marketing and sales.

Complaints and Agent Conduct

Consumer complaints about specific agents or agent practices require special attention from the insurance company. The insurer should respond promptly to the consumer and conduct any necessary fact finding, audits, and disciplinary action as necessary to correct any agent misconduct.

"If the recent investigations of MetLife, Prudential, and other companies is any indicator, there is clearly an increase in the amount of attention being paid to agent conduct," admits a representative from the NAIC. "While the state insurance departments have always been diligent in investigating complaints against agents, it is apparent that recently they are being more active and aggressive in such investigations." Regulators report that it is increasingly common for allegations of agent misconduct from consumer complaints to trigger at least a "targeted" market conduct examination.

"Most states will assure a third-party complainant, such as a contract holder, that a remedy will be provided by the insurer (which most courts will also find)," says Martin Wilson, former deputy insurance commissioner in Georgia. "Peculiar states like Alabama will hold an insurer liable to the full extent that an agent can be found liable. This would even include instances in which the agent clearly exceeded the scope of the agency and the insurer either did not know or even have reason to know of the conduct of the agent. Many insurers in Alabama have suffered punitive damage verdicts because of agent misconduct which was completely unknown to the company. This is true even in instances in which the insurer attempted to rectify the situation fully upon discovery of the agent misconduct."

Internal Compliance Audits: Preventive Medicine

By conducting compliance audits, or "practice" market conduct exams at the home office, many of the nightmares of a market conduct exam can be avoided. Highly recommended are:

- ✔ "unannounced" compliance audits
- ✔ random periodic customer surveys conducted by compliance personnel to check up on activities of the field force
- ✔ a company-wide, centralized complaint-handling database
- ✔ reporting systems that identify agents who exceed limits on replacements, policy lapses, duplicative sales, etc.

The senior officers and board members of an insurance company should routinely be made aware of the findings of internal audits. And companies should be prepared to discipline any field representatives or home office employees who are found violating ethical standards — regardless of their sales volume, level of productivity, or position in the organization.

"The best a company can do today is be sure it has good internal procedures for surveillance," observes ACLI's Dawson. "Clearly some of the most significant changes made by home offices has been the recent very heavy emphasis on the creation of internal assessment and supervision programs. This was one of the driving forces behind the ACLI's own adoption of an ethical market conduct program which features a very definite system of criteria by which a company would judge itself in its ability to monitor and govern many aspects of the sales and marketing process, not only confined to agents and agent activities."

The ACLI in 1996 adopted a program of self-assessment and third-party assessment for its member companies which is open to all life insurers.. The program establishes standards for ethical conduct, based on a set of six principles, to be voluntarily adopted by life insurers.

The principles include pledging to:

- ✔ Conduct business according to high standards of honesty and fairness
- ✔ Provide competent and customer-focused sales and service
- ✔ Engage in active and fair competition
- ✔ Provide advertising and sales materials that are clear and fair
- ✔ Provide for fair and efficient handling of customer complaints and disputes
- ✔ Maintain a reasonably designed system of supervision and review to achieve compliance with these principles

A questionnaire was designed to help insurers assess their compliance. Many of ACLI's member companies have already indicated an interest in participating in the rigorous self-assessment as well as the third party assessment required by the program, reports Dawson.

"Good internal surveillance programs are also important on account of the interest on the part of rating agencies to judge a company's creditworthiness based on such factors as their capacity to withstand lawsuits and regulatory scrutiny," adds Dawson.

✔ Check Your Understanding

1. J&R Insurance Company is proud of its dividend paying history. It takes out an advertisement in the newspaper declaring "Our company has been paying a substantial dividend every year since 1900, even during the Great Depression. Our company's dividends are as good as guaranteed." What is wrong with J&R's advertisement?

2. Claire has noticed that 18 of the last 20 disability income insurance applications she's submitted to a certain insurance company have been declined. When she talks to the underwriter, he tells her in confidence that the company will no longer approve DI applications from men in certain zip codes (those with a large gay population). What is the company doing wrong?

3. Stephen has just been hired as a licensing administrator for ABC Insurance Company. During his training, he is instructed to order a background investigation at the same time as he files a written appointment with the state insurance department. What reasons might Stephen have to question this practice?

CHAPTER 5

THE INSURER'S RESPONSIBILITIES TO AGENTS

The insurance company has certain legal, regulatory, professional, and ethical responsibilities to its appointed agents. The company establishes the agent's employment contract, must permit the agent to act in accordance with the terms of the contract, and must recognize all of the provisions of that contract. The agency agreement should clearly establish the relationship between the agent and the company, including:

- ✔ Representation and advertising methods
- ✔ Fiduciary arrangements
- ✔ Status of binding authority
- ✔ Procedures for premium payment (emphasizing "no commingling" laws)
- ✔ Cancellation procedures if the relationship is terminated
- ✔ Processing and recordkeeping arrangements, and
- ✔ Any requirement for agent errors and omissions coverage

In addition, the company must pay the agent the compensation agreed upon in the contract, reimburse the agent for proper expenditures made on behalf of the principal, and indemnify the agent for any losses or damages suffered without fault on the part of the agent but occurring on account of the agency relationship.

Since the insurance company operates entirely though the people it employs (especially its agents), the direction and example must come from the company. Companies should establish visible senior management support for compliance from the home office management and personnel all the way through to agency operations.

Clear Compliance Directives

An insurance company's primary responsibility to its agents is to provide explicit guidelines for acceptable and unacceptable market practices. Agents should receive initial and ongoing compliance training which defines what is and is not permissible when the agent is in the field. In the past, agents were given great latitude in managing customer relationships without home office oversight, but regulators have made it clear that those days are over. Regardless of whether the company considers its agents to be "independent contractors," the government imposes strict oversight and supervisory responsibilities.

Insurance companies aren't fined $20 million because a single producer does something wrong. The regulators look for patterns of agent (mis)behavior. Some questions to consider:

- ✔ Does the company properly recruit, conduct background investigations, and provide adequate training for new agents?
- ✔ Does the company offer compliance training along with training in basic sales skills?
- ✔ Are producers encouraged to take industry ethics courses?
- ✔ Are there home office initiatives to encourage ethical selling?
- ✔ Does the home office or field office have its own code of ethics and has it been communicated to the field force?
- ✔ Does the home office monitor agent performance?
- ✔ Are agents supervised and provided with ongoing training?
- ✔ Do the agents understand the technicalities of the products they sell?
- ✔ How are customer complaints against agents handled?
- ✔ How does the company respond when allegations of unethical practices are made?

"The way around the control problem is to be very clear about your company's philosophy about compliance," advises Andrew Salmon of the Texas Insurance Department's department of consumer protection.

Kay Doughty, the former Massachusetts insurance commissioner who now helps insurance companies prepare for market conduct exams, tries to emphasize the importance of good communication with the field force. "It's important to get agent input, and get agent buy-in" into any new compliance effort, says Doughty. Too often, she says, agents see company compliance crackdowns as attempts to squelch their ability to sell.

General Guidelines

Many insurers have established general guidelines for ethical employee and agent conduct. Commonly those guidelines address confidentiality, conflicts of interest, and legal and regulatory compliance.

Confidential Information

Confidential information obtained in the course of employment should not be used for an employee's personal gain or benefit. For example an employee should treat as confidential all information regarding the insurer's investment activities or plans. It is a violation of federal law for an employee or agent to trade in company securities on the basis of inside information which is acquired during the course of employment.

Conflicts of Interest

Employees and agents should avoid actual or apparent conflicts of interest — that is, a personal interest outside the company which could be placed ahead of the individual's obligation to the insurer. For example, most insurers will prohibit any employee or agent from serving as a director, officer, partner, or trustee in any outside business enterprise. An exception to this could be a family-held business.

Outsider Interest

Most companies prohibit their personnel from having any substantial interest or investment in an outside business which is involved with any business transaction with the insurer. This could also be viewed as a conflict of interest.

Gifts

Most insurers do not permit their employees to accept or provide any gifts or favors which might influence decisions involving business transactions. Even a nominal gift might appear to be influential with regard to business transactions (and could be construed as a violation of anti-rebating laws).

Insurers implement policies for the purpose of providing strict compliance with all civil and insurance laws and regulations. These company policies are aimed at good faith efforts on the part of employees to follow the spirit and intent of the law. Included in this compliance function, are prohibitions against gifts of value to government officials of both this country and foreign countries.

Conflicts Uncovered

A Pennsylvania agent received a 24-month license revocation and 3 years of future supervision for selling insurance to employees of the Center Township Water Authority, where he was employed.

This was considered a violation of the Ethics Commission's Ethics Act.

These policies are designed to place the insurer in a position to serve as a role model and leader regarding their ethical conduct. In turn, the insurer's employees and agents are expected to follow the lead of the company.

Written Compliance Plans

Many companies make it easier to comply with legal and ethical trade practices by providing agents with company manuals articulating corporate compliance policies. Companies have established entire compliance departments which control the creation, review, distribution, and use of all advertising materials. Compliance personnel train agents to educate the consumer, and require them to attend meetings to learn compliance and advertising standards.

Primerica Financial Services, (PFS) has a written ethics and compliance plan which outlines company policies, standards, and procedures, and assigns responsibility and authority for compliance from the home office through the field force. Company representatives, especially "regional vice presidents" (RVPs) and registered principals, are given "additional compliance leadership" monitoring and supervisory responsibilities with regard to the agents they oversee. RVPs are provided with a compliance guide, then must:

- ✔ Annually review the compliance program
- ✔ Certify that they have conducted required training of the agents they oversee
- ✔ Hold an annual compliance meeting, and
- ✔ Maintain all compliance materials and make them available to "downline" agents

The PFS Compliance plan addresses:

- ✔ General standards of conduct
- ✔ Licensing
- ✔ Product compliance
- ✔ New representative screening
- ✔ Training
- ✔ Publications (including an advertising handbook for use in the field)
- ✔ Compensation
- ✔ Underwriting
- ✔ Claims

- ✔ Field communications
- ✔ Complaint handling
- ✔ Reporting of misconduct, and
- ✔ Monitoring and enforcement

Agent Support and Training

The insurance company should provide for excellence in the recruiting, training, and ongoing support of its agents not just as part of its obligations to consumers but as part of its responsibilities towards its own agents. Agents deserve a fair chance to succeed in the insurance industry, and in many cases this depends on the quality of training and education provided by the principal. Industry experts have suggested strong mentoring programs as a good step to attracting the best and brightest. Others recommend that detailed training programs that last six months, a year, or even two years are necessary before an agent is ready to work alone.

Agent training often begins before the agent is contracted or hired by the company. This training is generally referred to as pre-contract training. It is primarily product and sales training designed to provide the new agent with a sales approach and a general working knowledge of the company's products.

This training is continued once the agent is placed under contract with the insurer. There is the need for continued sales and product training. In addition, the insurer will often encourage continued professional education through such industry associations as the Life Underwriting Training Council, and the Chartered Property/Casualty Underwriter and Chartered Life Underwriter programs available through the American College and American Institutes.

Some companies strongly support technical and continuing education, even going so far as to reimburse agents who attend continuing education seminars, or who enroll in educational courses and professional designation programs. Other companies believe that the responsibility for professional development lies with the agent himself or herself, and only provide for training during the agent's first few months or years of service. But continuing education is important, particularly with regard to new products and new regulatory requirements.

Agent Education Needs Greater Attention

"The education of agents is an area that needs greater attention," says John Mancini, market affairs manager for the NAIC.

"Many agents take prelicensing courses prior to licensure, but very quickly forget all that was learned about trade practices and market conduct regulations. Company training many times focuses on the sales process and product training and overlooks these issues.

"As part of its continuing education requirement, a state could require a course on trade practices, claims settlement practices, and market conduct, to increase agent understanding of these issues."

Many state regulations include agent training/notification requirements as part of the insurance company's responsibilities. During a market conduct examination, regulators may review all bulletins, memos, and newsletters used to communicate with the field force to ensure that producers are kept informed of new products, rates, rules, regulations, and company policies. For example, the new model law on life insurance policy illustrations requires the insurance carrier to certify that its agents have been made aware of the method the company uses to allocate policy expenses.

It is also the insurer's responsibility to train and develop quality sales managers, who influence and guide the field force on a daily basis through training and sales support. If the agents are to survive in the insurance business and possess necessary professional and ethical characteristics, the development of sales managers by the company is critical. Often, agent failure and agent problems are the result of poor field management. Proper agent and management training can produce the desired behavior and ethical conduct expected of the agents by the company and contribute to agent retention and success. Poor agent retention has always been a problem for the industry. Agents who are successful will stay in the business. Adequate training and management programs can enhance the agent's chances for success and survival in the business.

Home offices should insist that agents follow direction on regulatory matters and should provide assistance when needed in compliance. For example, many home offices will help agents correctly complete state-required disclosure and replacement forms.

During the multi-state investigation of the sales practices at Prudential, interviews with the sales force revealed that many agents were unaware of or confused about the company's replacement guidelines. The multi-state task force's executive summary noted "little if any consistency in agent training and agent awareness of company and regulatory guidelines."

Clear Sales Materials

In the wake of million dollar settlements based on policyholder claims of agent misconduct, many companies have become much more concerned about the sales process and have beefed up their compliance departments. Special attention has been given to the sales materials used in the field, and many companies now require a "control number" indicating home office approval before any sales document may be used. Also, pre-approved client letter types may be provided to the agent, giving specific examples of what can be said.

During a market conduct examination, examiners may review all forms of advertising and sales materials; whether designed for print or broadcast distribution, as well as materials used to train producers for sales presentations.

Examiners will determine whether advertising and sales materials accurately represent the policies being advertised and do not misrepresent or mislead policyholders by failing to disclose limitations or exclusions or by using misleading or ambiguous terminology. All sales materials must disclose the insurer's name and address and comply with state laws and regulations. Examiners will also determine whether the company allows its producers to create their own sales materials, and if so, whether it reviews and approves the sales materials and advertising prepared by its producers.

Fair Commission Structures

Unquestionably, one of the insurance company's primary responsibilities to agents is the payment of commissions. The whole insurance sales compensatory system revolves around commission earnings. The agent makes a sale and earns a commission. The sales manager may earn an override on the agent's commission. The company's regional vice president receives a bonus based on the production within his or her region. The measuring device for success is the number of sales made and the commissions earned. Sales pressure is exerted from the home office down to the field force for ever-increased and more profitable production.

While everyone agrees that "good" insurance agents are more concerned with their customers' needs and not focused on their own compensation, part of the problem is in the way the industry's commissions are structured. An agent's livelihood and potential for career advancement hinge on the ability to sell and meet sales quotas.

Unfortunately, the buyer may pay for this pressure when sales are made at the expense of his or her needs and objectives. The agent may conduct poor or incomplete fact finding and needs analysis. Out of financial desperation, an agent might resort to an unethical practice in an effort to make a sale and earn commissions. Quantity replaces quality service.

Incentives to Violate the Rules

The compensation of agents should be in proportion to the time and effort it takes to sell an insurance policy and meet regulatory requirements for underwriting and policy delivery.

The Need for Ongoing Service

One underlying (and incorrect) assumption is that the life insurance sales process is completed when the decision to purchase is made. The policy is stuck in a drawer and never consulted again.

Agents and their clients must understand that changing circumstances require modifications and adjustments to the life insurance policy over time.

The client may need or be able to afford more coverage, his or her protection goals may change, interest rates and values may not be performing as projected; all require ongoing monitoring and reconsideration.

Current commission structures do not support that level of continuing customer service.

Experimenting with Levelized Commissions

Acacia Mutual Life Insurance was among the first to introduce a levelized-type commission structure and reports having experienced improvements in both policy persistency and agent recruitment.

Early in 1996, State Farm gave its 17,000 exclusive agents the option of working under a new contract designed to reward multiline sales and business retention. The new agreement provides for smaller first year commissions on life insurance sales, but higher commissions in subsequent, renewal years to encourage continued client service. For personal lines insurance, compensation can be increased by the achievement of quality and retention goals.

First year commissions in life insurance are higher than renewal commission in recognition of the sometimes lengthy application process. These higher commissions in life insurance sales also are intended to improve agent retention by helping new agents survive the early, difficult years in the business and give them the incentive to locate new business.

But by paying higher commissions "up front" for "new business" companies effectively give agents an incentive for violating fair practices rules such as those prohibiting unnecessary policy replacement.

For example, a life agent's commission on the first year of a life insurance policy commonly runs 55% to 80% of the first year's premium, followed by renewal commissions at 5-10% of premium, eventually (usually after 10 years) dropping to 2%.

Documents provided by the insurance companies intended to facilitate an annual review of client's policy, listing information such as customer name, address, and amount of cash value in the current policy, have instead facilitated churning practices. Agents could easily identify policies with sufficient cash value to purchase a new policy and generate new commissions. And while not necessarily encouraging such behavior, many insurers looked the other way as policies were replaced.

Possible Alternatives

If the agent was assured of a paycheck regardless of actual sales results, might there be better service rendered to the buyer? Might there be fewer ethical violations? It has been argued that eliminating the current commission structures and substituting a salary might attract a more dedicated, committed individual to the insurance business. Sales could still be the primary motivation but the agent would also be rewarded for providing service to the client. This type of financial arrangement might also provide for better retention among agents and lower costs and expenses to the insurer.

Companies are beginning to reexamine their commission arrangements and make some changes. Alternative approaches include "levelized" commissions have which "even out" the high first policy year commissions and those of subsequent renewal years. They would have the added benefit of assuring (especially long-term) agents a steadier income stream. "Asset-based" compensation pays virtually nothing in the early years of a life insurance policy with higher amounts payable as the cash value builds.

In 1995 Prudential announced a change in how its life agents are compensated. Under the new system, a policy that remains in force for at least eight years will pay a higher commission than a standard "up front" policy, giving agents an incentive to keep existing policies in force (and keep providing policyholder service) rather than sell replacement policies.

The commission restructure was implemented ostensibly to improve policy persistency, but a beneficial side effect is that it is expected to help curb abusive sales practices. So far, the levelized commissions apply only to universal life policies with a $1 million or higher face amount, but similar changes are expected with other life products.

Other companies resist attempts to tamper with agent commissions, complaining that commissions are an "easy target" for reform, and that ethical agents aren't the ones giving poor service and improperly replacing policies. They argue that insurance companies should be allowed to choose whatever compensation systems suit them best in order to attract high quality insurance professionals.

Regulatory Attention

Several state insurance departments have also turned their attention to agent commission structures. Various state laws limit commissions paid on replacement policies, especially in the types of insurance sold to the elderly (Medicare supplement and long term care insurance, for example). The New York Insurance Department held a public hearing on agent compensation in October 1995, and intends to modernize laws regulating life insurance agent compensation.

Summary

The bottom line is that the insurer is always held accountable, at least financially, for the actions of its agents; to what extent the insurer is held accountable differs from state to state. It is in the insurer's own best interest to develop, communicate, and enforce clear compliance directives for its field force, to provide adequate agent support and training, to provide fair advertising materials, and encourage ethical behavior through fair commission structures.

Commission Disclosure

There is a growing consumer movement that is also receiving regulatory attention: commission disclosure.

The feeling is that consumers are better informed if they also understand how much the insurance agent makes from each insurance transaction, just as home buyers and sellers understand how much the real estate agent makes from the sale/purchase of a house.

Such a requirement is already in effect in other countries such as Australia and the United Kingdom. However, the U.S. insurance industry isn't quite ready for that large of a step. After heavy pressure from the life insurance industry, a provision requiring commission disclosure was dropped from the NAIC's life policy illustrations model act.

✔ Check Your Understanding

1. Ginger has just passed her agent licensing exam and landed a great job with the ABC Agency. Her first day on the job she is handed two insurance policies and a printout of 200 leads. She is told her goal is to "close" at least 20 policies in her first month. Identify what additional training the agency should provide before Ginger starts soliciting customers.

2. Describe how current agent commission structures can contribute to the failure to support continuing customer service.

3. Respond to the comment, "An insurance company that considers its agents independent contractors doesn't have to worry about training the field force."

CONCLUSION

While the insurance industry has never enjoyed high public approval ratings, the damage sustained by the industry over the market conduct crisis is incalculable. Clearly, industry efforts to help restore public confidence are in order.

Industry reforms that will help resolve the market conduct crisis include:

- ✔ Ethics training
- ✔ Sales force oversight
- ✔ Due diligence in agent recruiting and training
- ✔ Internal compliance audits
- ✔ More sophisticated reporting systems and complaint handling procedures
- ✔ Clear sales materials
- ✔ Information sharing
- ✔ Illustration reform
- ✔ Fair commission structures

What can agents do to be sure they are fulfilling absolutely all of their compliance responsibilities?

- ✔ Complying with terms of agency contracts
- ✔ Continuing their education in products, ethics, law and industry changes
- ✔ Maintaining technical expertise
- ✔ Conducting thorough needs analysis and fact finding
- ✔ Submitting accurate and complete policy applications
- ✔ Maintaining confidentiality of client information
- ✔ Performing all disclosure as required
- ✔ Performing all necessary policyholder service and annual reviews
- ✔ Maintaining accurate and complete documentation and recordkeeping
- ✔ Keeping licenses and appointments current
- ✔ Conducting internal reviews

- ✔ Using only approved sales materials, advertising, illustrations, and presentations

Clearly, the essence of market conduct starts with the agent, who must be both a responsible and responsive professional. The future of the insurance business and the developing nature of market conduct will continue to be shaped by each individual agent, as well as timely industry reforms.

FINAL COURSE REVIEW

1. Using misleading tactics to persuade consumers to replace existing life insurance policies and use the cash value to purchase new coverage with the same comapny is a practice known as:

   A. canvasing.
   B. cold-lead advertising.
   C. churning.
   D. competition.

2. In an insurance sales presentation, which party would be the "principal"?

   A. The consumer.
   B. The insurance company.
   C. The agent.
   D. The regulatory authority.

3. Each of the following is true when an insurance company uses a celebrity testimonial in its advertising except:

   A. The advertising must indicate if the person giving the testimonial is being paid.
   B. The advertising must indicate whether the person giving the testimonial has any financial interest in the company.
   C. The testimonial given must relate to the policy being advertised.
   D. The person giving the testimonial must not make any testimonials for competing insurance companies.

4. Which of the following best describes the nature of "market conduct" examinations?

   A. Analysis of interest rate trends and how these affect insurance benefits payable to consumers.
   B. Examination of the non-financial business practices and operations of insurers and their agents.
   C. Investigation into the investment practices of insurance companies.
   D. Hearings held to determine whether requested rate increases are justified.

5. The authority of an insurance agent, as spelled out in the agency contract with an insurance company, is known as:

   A. express authority.
   B. presumed authority.
   C. apparent authority.
   D. implied authority.

6. Which of the following is most likely to have the authority to bind insurance coverages?

   A. An insurance solicitor.
   B. An insurance broker.
   C. A life and health insurance agent.
   D. A property and casualty insurance agent.

7. An agency contract or agreement between an insurance agent and insurance company is likely to specify all of the following except:

   A. the agent's obligation to members of the public.
   B. the contract expiration or renewal date.
   C. the extent of the agent's authority to act for the insurer.
   D. the identity of the parties to the contract.

8. The primary purpose of compliance directives issued by an insurance company to its agents should be to:

   A. establish written disclaimers that will protect the company against any later charges of wrongdoing.
   B. create favorable publicity relating to its expressed concern for consumers.
   C. provide agents with explicit guidelines for acceptable and unacceptable market practices.
   D. satisfy the Insurance Department that it has made a minimum effort to control market conduct.

9. Generally, the term "fiduciary" means a person who:

   A. represents another party in a transaction.
   B. has a state license reflecting professional competence.
   C. is in a position of financial trust.
   D. has a written agreement to provide services in exchange for a specified fee.

10. Pretext interviews are generally prohibited in the insurance business, except in cases where:

    A. there appears to be evidence of criminal activity or fraud.
    B. the agent is engaging in legitimate field underwriting.
    C. advance permission has been obtained from the principal to conduct a pretext interview.
    D. the person interviewed agrees to provide information without knowing the purpose of the interview.

11. In most states, the responsibility for qualifying new agents prior to appointment falls primarily on:

    A. the state insurance department.
    B. the consumer affairs division of the state government.
    C. the insurance company sponsoring the agent.
    D. the professional agent associations in the area.

12. Which of the following behaviors on the part of an insurance company would be most likely to result in sanctions and penalties?

    A. Random violations of the insurance law or regulations.
    B. Premium billing errors attributed to a new employee who was not properly trained.
    C. An isolated incident of misconduct by an agent representing the company.
    D. A pattern suggesting that repeated violations are a general business practice.

13. The primary objective of an insurance agent when engaging in field underwriting should be to:

    A. obtain the lowest available rate for the applicant.
    B. advise the applicant on how to avoid revealing any negative information on the application.
    C. protect the insurance company from adverse risks.
    D. enhance opportunities for completion of the sales transaction.

14. What distinguishes the practice of "twisting" from the practice of "churning"?

    A. Twisting involves an external replacement while churning involves an internal replacement.
    B. Churning involves an external replacement while twisting involves an internal replacement.
    C. Replacement transactions resulting in a lower premium are known as twisting, and those resulting in a higher premium are known as churning.
    D. Twisting and churning are synonymous and have the same meaning in all cases.

15. Which term best describes the process of selection, classification, and rating of insurable risks?

    A. Auditing.
    B. Commingling.
    C. Binding.
    D. Underwriting.

16. The cost of a market conduct examination is usually borne by:

    A. the insurance company being examined.
    B. the insurance department conducting the examination.
    C. the general revenue fund of the state which is conducting the examination.
    D. consumers through surcharges on policies which are affected by the examination.

17. A false statement made in writing on an application for insurance would be an example of:

    A. contract formation.
    B. fiduciary duties.
    C. concealment.
    D. misrepresentation.

18. Making maliciously critical or derogatory statements about another insurer with the intent to cause injury is an example of a practice known as:

    A. discrimination.
    B. boycott or intimidation.
    C. defamation.
    D. cold lead advertising.

19. When a market conduct examination reveals wrongdoing, which of the following presents the greatest potential financial threat to the insurance company committing violations?

    A. Fines imposed by the insurance department.
    B. Class action lawsuits seeking damages.
    C. Administrative penalties under state law.
    D. Negative publicity.

20. Which of the following best describes an internal compliance audit?

    A. A practice market conduct exam conducted by an insurance company to discover its own shortcomings.
    B. A market conduct exam conducted by the insurance department when wrongdoing is suspected.
    C. Filing financial reports as required in order to comply with existing insurance regulations.
    D. Special training given to company employees and agents concerning their ethical obligations.

21. In which of the following cases might it be proper for an agent to propose the replacement of an existing life insurance policy?

    A. When the existing policy has more favorable policy loan interest rates.
    B. When the replacement policy has the same face amount as the existing policy and a higher premium.
    C. When the replacement policy has a lower face amount than the existing policy and the same premium.
    D. When the existing policy does not meet the current needs of the consumer.

22. What is the primary purpose of the statutory limitation on the writing of "controlled business" by insurance agents?

    A. To prohibit agents from writing coverages that insure illegal activities or benefit criminal interests.
    B. To require agents to do business with members of the public, and not use the license mainly to receive commissions on their own insurance coverages.
    C. To verify that all applicants for insurance coverages have a legitimate insurable interest.
    D. To promote competition between insurance companies and prevent any one company from establishing a monopoly.

23. Insurance laws prohibit various forms of unfair discrimination against insurance applicants, but discrimination may be permitted when it is based on:

    A. an underwriter's experience with particular risks.
    B. information verified by an investigative report.
    C. geographic location of the risk.
    D. sound actuarial principles.

24. Which of the following is not one of the possible negative consequences for a consumer who replaces an existing health insurance policy with another?

    A. The new policy may establish a new period excluding coverage for any preexisting conditions.
    B. The new policy may provide higher benefit amounts and lower deductibles than the old policy.
    C. The new policy may establish new waiting periods before benefits become payable.
    D. The new policy may not cover some losses which would have been covered by the old policy due to differences in general exclusions.

25. What is meant by the term "pre-contract training"?

    A. Sales training focusing on sales presentation techniques prior to presenting an application form.
    B. Special training focusing on completing applications prior to acceptance of the risk by the insurer.
    C. Initial training of proposed agents before they are hired or given agency contracts.
    D. Company training of sales managers who will guide the field force and provide on-going sales support.

FINAL COURSE REVIEW ANSWER SHEET

1 Ⓐ Ⓑ Ⓒ Ⓓ
2 Ⓐ Ⓑ Ⓒ Ⓓ
3 Ⓐ Ⓑ Ⓒ Ⓓ
4 Ⓐ Ⓑ Ⓒ Ⓓ
5 Ⓐ Ⓑ Ⓒ Ⓓ
6 Ⓐ Ⓑ Ⓒ Ⓓ
7 Ⓐ Ⓑ Ⓒ Ⓓ
8 Ⓐ Ⓑ Ⓒ Ⓓ
9 Ⓐ Ⓑ Ⓒ Ⓓ
10 Ⓐ Ⓑ Ⓒ Ⓓ
11 Ⓐ Ⓑ Ⓒ Ⓓ
12 Ⓐ Ⓑ Ⓒ Ⓓ
13 Ⓐ Ⓑ Ⓒ Ⓓ
14 Ⓐ Ⓑ Ⓒ Ⓓ
15 Ⓐ Ⓑ Ⓒ Ⓓ
16 Ⓐ Ⓑ Ⓒ Ⓓ
17 Ⓐ Ⓑ Ⓒ Ⓓ
18 Ⓐ Ⓑ Ⓒ Ⓓ
19 Ⓐ Ⓑ Ⓒ Ⓓ
20 Ⓐ Ⓑ Ⓒ Ⓓ
21 Ⓐ Ⓑ Ⓒ Ⓓ
22 Ⓐ Ⓑ Ⓒ Ⓓ
23 Ⓐ Ⓑ Ⓒ Ⓓ
24 Ⓐ Ⓑ Ⓒ Ⓓ
25 Ⓐ Ⓑ Ⓒ Ⓓ

FINAL COURSE REVIEW ANSWER KEY

1	A	B	●	D
2	A	●	C	D
3	A	B	C	●
4	A	●	C	D
5	●	B	C	D
6	A	B	C	●
7	●	B	C	D
8	A	B	●	D
9	A	B	●	D
10	●	B	C	D
11	A	B	●	D
12	A	B	C	●
13	A	B	●	D
14	●	B	C	D
15	A	B	C	●
16	●	B	C	D
17	A	B	C	●
18	A	B	●	D
19	A	●	C	D
20	●	B	C	D
21	A	B	C	●
22	A	●	C	D
23	A	B	C	●
24	A	●	C	D
25	A	B	●	D

RESOURCES APPENDIX

Agents' Legal Responsibility, Ronald T. Anderson PhD, CPCU, CLU, National Underwriter Co., Cincinnati OH 45202.

Are You in Compliance; the Business Standards Ethics Committee, Houston Association of Life Underwriters; available from LIMRA International, P.O. Box 208, Hartford CT 06141-0208 (800) 688-3358.

The Changing Nature of Insurance Regulation, Karen L. Hamilton, Insurance Institute of America, 720 Providence Road, Malvern PA 19355-0770 (610) 544-2100.

The Choice is Yours, A Guide to Selecting Quality Producers, LIMRA International.

Code of Professional Ethics of the American Institute for Chartered Property Casualty Underwriters, American Institute for CPCU, 720 Providence Road, Malvern PA 19355-0716 (610) 644-2100.

Compliance: The Life Insurance Practitioner's Practical Survival Guide, Dennis M. Groner PhD, CLU, ChFC, and Mary B. Petersen JD, CLU, ChFC, Leimberg Associates Books, Bryn Mawr PA 19010.

Ethics: Piecing Together the Ethical Puzzle; LUTC, 7625 Wisconsin Ave., Bethesda MD 20814 (301) 913-5882.

The Market Conduct Examiners Handbook, National Association of Insurance Commissioners, 120 W. 12th Street, Kansas City MO 84105 (816) 842-3600.

On Professions, Professionals, and Professional Ethics, Ronald C. Horn, American Institute for CPCU.

Perspectives of Insurance Regulation, Karen L. Hamilton, Insurance Institute of America.

The Regulation of Insurance, Justin L. Brady, Joyce Hall Mellinger, Kenneth N. Scoles Jr, Insurance Institute of America.

Replacement Questionnaires, American Society of CLU & ChFC, 270 Bryn Mawr Avenue, Bryn Mawr PA 19010 (800) 392-6900.

The Retail Sales Practices of Life Insurance Companies: Compliance and Litigation in the 1990s, Mahlon M. Frankhauser, Thomas Tew, Prentice Hall Law & Business, Englewood Cliffs NJ.

Selling Ethically: How Do I Benefit?, LIMRA International.

State Insurance Regulation, Kathleen Heald Ettlinger, Karen L. Hamilton, Gregory Krohm, Insurance Institute of America.

The Trusted Advisor, LIMRA International.